THE CRETE ADVENTURE: A TRAVEL PREPARATION GUIDE

SHONDA WILLIAMS

All rights reserved. No part of this publication may be reproduced, distributed, or transmitted in any form or by any means, including photocopying, recording, or other electronic or mechanical methods, without the prior written permission of the publisher, except in the case of brief quotations embodied in critical reviews and certain other noncommercial uses permitted by copyright law.
Copyright © (SHONDA WILLIAMS) (2024).

All images in this book are from pexels.com

Table of Contents

Introduction	**9**
Chapter 1 • Welcome to Crete	**13**
Brief History of Crete	13
Why Visit Crete?	18
Chapter 2 • Planning Your Trip	**21**
Best Time to Visit Crete	21
Getting to and around Crete	23
Currency and Money Matters	26
Accommodation Options	30
Chapter 3 • Cretan Culture and Etiquette	**35**
Cretan Language and Basic Phrases	35
Cultural Norms and Customs	39
Dining Etiquette	43
Dress Code and Fashion in Crete	44
Festivals and Celebrations	50
Chapter 4 • Exploring Crete	**55**
Chania	55
Rethymno	57
Heraklion	59
Lasithi	61
Chapter 5 • Top Attractions	**65**
The Palace of Knossos	65
Agios Nikolaos	67
Samaria Gorge	69
Heraklion Archaeological Museum	71
Preveli Monastery and Preveli Beach	74

Matala Beach	76
Diktaion (Psychro) Cave	78

Chapter 6 • Accommodation Recommendations   **81**

Villa Recommendations	81
Hotel Recommendations	85
Guesthouse Recommendations	87

Chapter 7 • Cretan Cuisine and Food Experiences   **91**

Introduction to Cretan Cuisine	91
Famous Cretan Dishes	92
Famous Cretan Drinks	98
Wine and Food Pairing	102
Must-Visit Cretan Restaurants and Cafes	105
Culinary Experiences and Cooking Classes	110

Chapter 8 • Outdoor Activities and Nature   **113**

Hiking and Trekking in Crete	113
WaterSports in Crete	118
Horse riding in Crete	121
Kitesurfing in Crete	124
Canyoning in Crete	127
Climbing and Caving in Crete	129
Wellness: Spas, Retreats, and Yoga	134

Chapter 9 • Shopping in Crete   **143**

Fashion and Luxury Shopping	143
Local Markets and Souvenirs	148
Artisan Crafts and Workshops	151

Chapter 10 • Practical Information   **157**

Health and Safety Tips	157
Emergency Contacts	160

Communication and Internet Access	165
Chapter 11 • Recommended Itineraries	**171**
One day in Crete	171
Three days in Crete	172
Five days in Crete	175
Chapter 12 • Travelling with Children	**179**
Child-Friendly Attractions	179
Child-Friendly Accommodation	184
Chapter 13 • Travelling on a Budget	**187**
Budget-Friendly Accommodation	187
Cheap Eats and Local Food	189
Free and Affordable Attractions	192
Transportation Tips for Saving Money	197
Chapter 14 • Day Trips and Excursions	**203**
Santorini	203
Kythira	207
Elounda	211

Chapter 15 • Sustainability and Responsible Travel 213

Conclusion	**219**

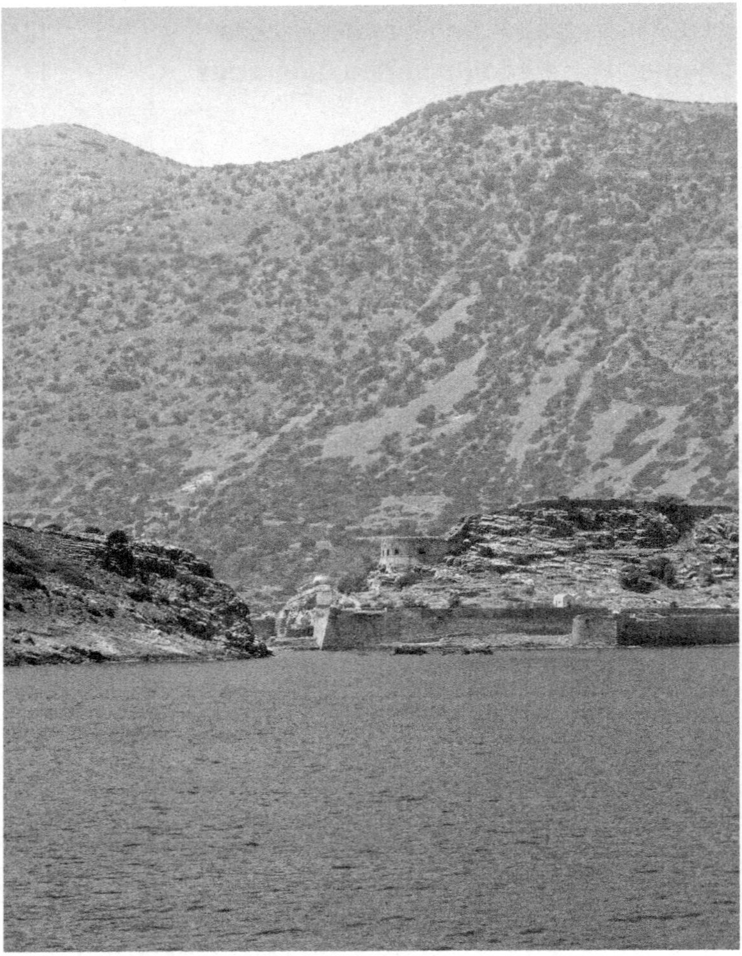

Introduction

Crete is more than just an island. It is a world of its own, where ancient history, diverse culture, stunning nature, and delicious cuisine blend to create an unforgettable experience for every visitor. Whether you are looking for a relaxing beach holiday, an adventurous hiking trip, a cultural exploration, or a gastronomic delight, Crete has something for everyone.

In this travel guide, you will find all the information you need to plan your perfect trip to Crete. You will learn about the best places to visit, the most interesting things to do, the most comfortable places to stay, and the most practical tips to make your journey smooth and enjoyable. You will also discover the rich history and culture of Crete, from the Minoan civilization to the modern day, and the unique traditions and customs that make the island so special.

Crete is the largest and most populous of the Greek islands, located in the southern Aegean Sea. It has four administrative regions: Chania, Rethymno, Heraklion, and Lassithi, each with its distinctive character and attractions. The northern coast of Crete is more developed and touristy, while the southern coast is more secluded and authentic. The island has a varied landscape, ranging from sandy beaches and rocky coves to fertile plains and rugged mountains. Crete is also home to some of the most impressive natural wonders in Greece, such as the **Samaria Gorge**, the **Balos Lagoon**, and the **Elafonisi Beach**.

Crete is not only a place of natural beauty, but also a place of historical significance and cultural heritage. It is the birthplace of Zeus, the king of the Greek gods, and the site of the legendary Minotaur's labyrinth. It is the cradle of the Minoan civilization, one of the oldest and most advanced in Europe, and the witness of many invasions and occupations, from the Romans and the Byzantines to the Venetians and the Ottomans. It is the land of brave heroes and proud rebels, who fought for their freedom and identity against foreign oppressors. It is the source of inspiration for many artists and writers, such as **Nikos Kazantzakis**, the author of Zorba the Greek.

Crete is also a place of culinary excellence, where the Mediterranean diet is at its best. The island's cuisine is based on fresh, local, and organic ingredients, such as olive oil, cheese, honey, herbs, vegetables, fruits, fish, and meat. The Cretan dishes are simple, yet flavorful and nutritious, reflecting the island's history and geography. Some of the most famous Cretan specialities are dakos (a salad of barley rusks, tomatoes, cheese, and oregano), kalitsounia (cheese or herb pies), snails (cooked in various ways), gamopilafo (rice with meat and broth), and raki (a strong alcoholic drink made from grapes).

Crete is a destination that will captivate you with its charm, diversity, and hospitality. It is a place where you can enjoy the sun, the sea, and the sand, but also explore the ancient ruins, the medieval castles, and the traditional villages. It is a place where you can taste delicious food, aromatic wine, and sweet pastries, but also experience the lively music, the colourful dances, and the festive celebrations. It is a place where you can relax, have fun, and learn, but also feel the spirit, the soul, and the heart of Crete.

This is the ultimate travel guide to Crete, the island of wonders. Welcome to Crete, and enjoy your stay!

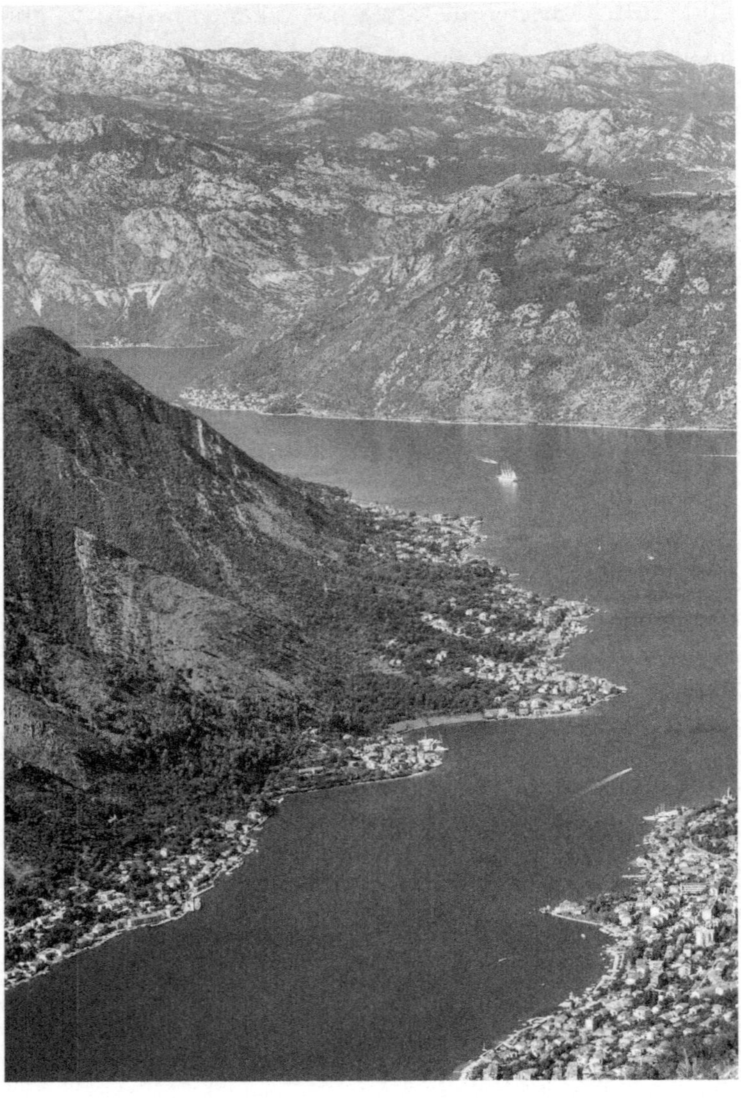

Chapter 1 • Welcome to Crete

Brief History of Crete

Crete is an island with a long and rich history, spanning from prehistoric times to the present day. It has witnessed the rise and fall of civilizations, the glory and tragedy of wars, the fusion and clash of cultures, and the evolution and preservation of traditions. Crete is a place where the past and the present coexist, creating a unique and fascinating identity.

The first traces of human presence on Crete date back to the Paleolithic era, more than 100,000 years ago, when hunter-gatherers crossed the sea from Asia or Africa. They were followed by the Neolithic farmers, who introduced domesticated animals and plants and established the first permanent settlements. The most remarkable and influential period of Crete's history, however, was the Bronze Age, when the Minoan civilization flourished.

The Minoans, named after their legendary king Minos, were the first advanced civilization in Europe, and one of the most sophisticated in the world. They built magnificent palaces, such as Knossos, Phaistos, and Malia, which served as administrative, religious, and economic centres. They developed a complex social and political system, a refined art and culture, a maritime trade network, and a mysterious writing system, known as Linear A, which remains undeciphered. They also worshipped nature and female deities, such as the Mother Goddess and the Snake Goddess.

The Minoan civilization reached its peak around 1600 BC, but soon after, it faced a series of disasters that led to its decline and collapse. Some of these disasters were natural, such as earthquakes, volcanic eruptions, and tsunamis, while others were human, such as invasions, wars, and rebellions. The most likely scenario is that a combination of these factors weakened the Minoan society, and made it vulnerable to the attacks of the Mycenaeans, a warlike people from mainland Greece, who conquered Crete around 1450 BC, and assimilated the Minoan culture.

The Mycenaean domination of Crete lasted for about two centuries, until the end of the Bronze Age, when another wave of invaders, the Dorians, arrived from the north. The Dorians brought with them the Iron Age technology, the Greek language, and the worship of the Olympian gods. They also divided the island into city-states, which competed and fought with each other for power and resources. This period of turmoil and fragmentation lasted for almost a millennium, until the arrival of a new power, the Romans.

The Romans annexed Crete in 67 BC, after a long and fierce resistance by the Cretans. They made the island a province of their empire and brought peace and prosperity. They built roads, aqueducts, theatres, temples, and villas, and introduced new crops, such as grapes and olives. They also spread Christianity, which became the official religion of the empire in the 4th century AD. The Roman rule of Crete lasted for about five centuries, until the division of the empire into two parts, the Western and the Eastern.

Crete became part of the Eastern Roman Empire, also known as the Byzantine Empire, which preserved the Greek language and culture, and the Christian faith. The Byzantines fortified the island against the raids of pirates and barbarians and built many churches and monasteries, some of which still survive today. They also faced internal conflicts and schisms, such as the Iconoclastic Controversy, which divided the church and the society over the use of religious images. The

Byzantine rule of Crete was interrupted twice by foreign occupations: the first by the Arabs, who founded the emirate of Crete in the 9th century, and the second by the Venetians, who bought the island from the Crusaders in the 13th century.

The Venetians ruled Crete for more than four centuries and left a lasting imprint on its architecture, economy, and culture. They transformed the island into a flourishing commercial and artistic hub and a bastion of their maritime empire. They built impressive fortifications, such as the walls of Heraklion and the fortress of Spinalonga, and elegant buildings, such as the Loggia and the Morosini Fountain. They also encouraged the development of literature, painting, and music, giving birth to the Cretan Renaissance, which produced famous artists, such as El Greco, Vitsentzos Kornaros, and Francesco Barozzi.

The Venetian rule of Crete was not peaceful, however, as the Cretans often rebelled against harsh taxation and social discrimination. The most serious threat to the Venetian domination, though, came from the Ottoman Empire, which had been expanding its power and influence in the eastern Mediterranean. The Ottomans besieged and conquered Crete, after a long and bloody war, which lasted from 1645 to 1669 and resulted in the loss of thousands of lives and the destruction of many monuments. The Ottomans imposed their religion, law, and administration, and converted many churches into mosques, such as the Agios Titos and the Agia Sofia.

The Ottoman rule of Crete was also marked by frequent uprisings and revolts, as the Cretans struggled for their freedom and independence. Some of these revolts were supported by foreign powers, such as Russia, France, and Britain, who had interests in the region. The most significant revolt was the Cretan Revolution of 1866-1869, which was inspired by the Greek War of Independence of 1821-1830, and aimed at the union of Crete with Greece. The revolution failed, but it raised the awareness and the sympathy of the European public opinion and paved the way for the future liberation of Crete.

The final stage of the Cretan struggle for independence was the Cretan War of 1897-1898, which was triggered by the massacre of hundreds of Cretans by the Ottoman troops in Heraklion. The war involved the intervention of the Great Powers, who imposed an autonomous regime on Crete, under their protection and the suzerainty of the Ottoman Empire. The first governor of the autonomous Crete was Prince George of Greece, who faced the opposition of the Cretan rebels, who demanded full union with Greece. The union was finally achieved in 1913, after the Balkan Wars, which ended the Ottoman presence in the Balkans.

Crete became an integral part of the modern Greek state and participated in the national and international events that shaped the 20th century. Crete was involved in the World Wars, the Greek Civil War, the Cold War, and European integration. Crete also faced the challenges and the opportunities of economic and social development, urbanization and tourism, education and the ure, and the preservation and innovation of its identity. Crete is a place that has a lot to offer to its visitors, who can discover its history, its nature, its people, and its spirit. Crete is a place that will enchant you with its beauty, its diversity, and its hospitality. Crete is a place that you will love.

Why Visit Crete?

History and Culture: Crete is not only a place of natural beauty, but also a place of historical significance and cultural heritage. It is the birthplace of Zeus, the king of the Greek gods, and the site of the legendary

Minotaur's labyrinth. It is the cradle of the Minoan civilization, one of the oldest and most advanced in Europe, and the witness of many invasions and occupations, from the Romans and the Byzantines to the Venetians and the Ottomans. It is the land of brave heroes and proud rebels, who fought for their freedom and identity against foreign oppressors. It is the source of inspiration for many artists and writers, such as Nikos Kazantzakis, the author of Zorba the Greek.

Food: Crete is also a place of culinary excellence, where the Mediterranean diet is at its best. The island's cuisine is based on fresh, local, and organic ingredients, such as olive oil, cheese, honey, herbs, vegetables, fruits, fish, and meat. The Cretan dishes are simple, yet flavorful and nutritious, reflecting the island's history and geography. Some of the most famous Cretan specialities are dakos (a salad of barley rusks, tomatoes, cheese, and oregano), kalitsounia (cheese or herb pies), snails (cooked in various ways), gamopilafo (rice with meat and broth), and raki (a strong alcoholic drink made from grapes).

20

Chapter 2 • Planning Your Trip

Best Time to Visit Crete

Below are some factors to consider when choosing the best time to visit Crete:

Weather: Crete has a Mediterranean climate, with hot and dry summers and mild and wet winters. The average temperature ranges from 15°C (59°F) in January to 29°C (84°F) in July and August. The sea temperature varies from 16°C (61°F) in February to 26°C (79°F) in August. The island has four distinct regions: the north coast, the south coast, the central mountains, and the eastern plateau, each with its own microclimate and weather patterns. Generally, the north coast is more windy and humid, the south coast is more sunny and dry, the central mountains are cooler and snowier, and the eastern plateau is hotter and drier.

Crowds: Crete is a popular tourist destination, especially in the summer months, when the island is full of visitors from all over the world. The peak season is from June to mid-September when the prices are higher, the availability is lower, and the attractions are busier.

The shoulder seasons are from April to May and from mid-September to October when the crowds are smaller, the prices are lower, and the availability is higher. The low season is from November to March when the island is quiet, the prices are lowest, and the availability is highest, but many tourist facilities are closed or have limited hours.

Activities: Crete offers a wide range of activities for different interests and tastes. If you are interested in beach activities, such as swimming, sunbathing, snorkelling, or surfing, the best time to visit is from June to September, when the weather is warm and sunny, and the water is calm and clear. If you are interested in hiking activities, such as exploring the gorges, the mountains, or the countryside, the best time to visit is from April to June or from September to October, when the weather is mild and pleasant, and nature is green and blooming. If you are interested in cultural activities, such as visiting the archaeological sites, the museums, or the villages, the best time to visit is from April to October, when most of the attractions are open and accessible, and there are many festivals and events to enjoy.

In conclusion, the best time to visit Crete depends on

your personal preferences and expectations, but generally, the shoulder seasons of spring and autumn are the most ideal, as they offer a balance of good weather, moderate crowds, reasonable prices, and plenty of activities and attractions to enjoy. However, no matter when you visit, Crete will charm you with its beauty, diversity, and hospitality.

Getting to and around Crete

Getting to Crete is easy, as the island has three international airports: Heraklion, Chania, and Sitia. There are frequent flights from Athens and other major European cities, as well as seasonal charter flights from various destinations. You can also reach Crete by ferry from Piraeus, the main port of Athens, or from other islands, such as Santorini, Rhodes, or Cyprus. The ferry journey takes from 6 to 9 hours, depending on the route and the speed of the boat. You can book your tickets online or at the port.

Getting around Crete is a bit more challenging, as the island is huge and has many places to explore. However, there are several options to suit your preferences and budget, such as:

Car: Renting a car is the best way to get around Crete if you want to have the freedom and flexibility to visit any place at any time. You can find many car rental agencies at the airports, the ports, or the main towns, offering a variety of models and prices. You will need a valid driver's license and a credit card to rent a car. Driving in Crete is generally safe and easy, as the roads are well-maintained and signposted, although some rural roads may be narrow and winding. You should also be aware of the traffic rules and regulations, such as the speed limits, the parking zones, and the toll fees. The average cost of renting a car in Crete is around €30 per day.

Bus: Taking the bus is the cheapest and most eco-friendly way to get around Crete if you don't mind following a fixed schedule and sharing the ride with other passengers. There are two main bus companies in Crete: KTEL Hania-Rethymno, which covers the western part of the island, and KTEL Heraklion-Lassithi, which covers the central and eastern part. The buses are modern, comfortable, and air-conditioned, and connect all the major towns and attractions, as well as some remote villages and beaches. You can buy your tickets online, at the bus stations, or on board. The bus fares vary depending on the distance and the destination, but they are usually between €2 and €15.

Taxi: Taking a taxi is the most convenient and fastest way to get around Crete if you want to avoid the hassle of driving or waiting for the bus. You can find taxis at the airports, the ports, the bus stations, or the main squares, or you can call one by phone or use an app. The taxis are metered and have a standard rate per kilometer, which is higher at night and on holidays. You can also negotiate a fixed price for longer trips or special services, such as tours or transfers. The average cost of taking a taxi in Crete is around €1 per kilometer.

Ferry: Taking a ferry is the most scenic and relaxing way to get around Crete if you want to enjoy the views of the coast and the sea. There are several ferry companies that operate along the south and west coast of the island, linking the main ports, such as Hora Sfakion, Sougia, Paleohora, Agia Roumeli, and Kissamos, with the popular beaches, such as Loutro, Marmara, Glyka Nera, and Elafonisi. The ferries are small, wooden, and colorful, and have a capacity of up to 50 passengers. You can buy your tickets at the port or on board. The ferry fares vary depending on the distance and the destination, but they are usually between €5 and €20.

Bike: Riding a bike is the most adventurous and fun

way to get around Crete if you want to experience the nature and the culture of the island. You can find many bike rental agencies in the main towns, offering a variety of models and prices. You can also join a guided bike tour or a self-guided bike trip, which include accommodation, luggage transfer, and support. Riding a bike in Crete is challenging and rewarding, as the island has many hills, mountains, and gorges, as well as flat and scenic routes. You should also be prepared for the weather, the traffic, and the road conditions. The average cost of renting a bike in Crete is around €15 per day.

No matter which option you choose, getting around Crete will be an unforgettable experience, as the island has so much to offer to its visitors. You will discover its history, its culture, its nature, and its people, and you will fall in love with its beauty, its diversity, and its hospitality.

Currency and Money Matters

Crete is part of Greece, and therefore, the official currency is the Euro (€). The Euro is divided into 100 cents, and there are coins of 1, 2, 5, 10, 20, and 50 cents, as well as €1 and €2. The banknotes come in denominations of €5, €10, €20, €50, €100, €200, and €500, although the latter two are rarely used. You can check the current exchange rate of your currency to the Euro using our currency converter on the side.

There are several ways to obtain Euros in Crete, depending on your convenience and preference. Below are some of the most common options:

Cash: You can bring cash in your own currency and exchange it at banks, post offices, or bureau de change kiosks, which are found at the airports, the ports, and the main towns. You can also exchange cash at some hotels and tourist shops, but the rates may not be as favorable. The exchange rates vary depending on the market and the commission fees, so it is advisable to compare them before making a transaction. You should also keep the receipt of the exchange, as you may need it to reconvert your leftover Euros when you leave.

Credit/Debit Cards: You can use your credit or debit cards to withdraw cash from ATMs, which are widely available throughout the island. You can also use them to pay for goods and services at most hotels, restaurants, shops, and other establishments. However, you should be aware of the fees and charges that your card issuer may apply, such as transaction fees, conversion fees, or foreign exchange fees. You should also inform your bank before traveling to Crete, to avoid any problems with your card security or authorization. Moreover, you should always have some cash on hand, as some places may not accept cards or may have a minimum amount for card payments.

Travelers' Cheques: You can buy travelers' cheques in your own currency and cash them at banks, post offices, or bureau de change kiosks in Crete. You can also use them to pay for goods and services at some hotels, restaurants, shops, and other establishments, but you may need to show your passport and pay a commission fee. Travelers' cheques are a safe and convenient way to carry money, as they can be replaced if lost or stolen. However, they are not as widely accepted or used as cash or cards, and they may have a lower exchange rate than cash.

Prepaid Cards: You can buy prepaid cards in your own currency and load them with Euros before or during your trip. You can use them to withdraw cash from ATMs or to pay for goods and services at most places that accept cards. Prepaid cards are a secure and convenient way to manage your money, as they have a fixed amount and can be blocked if lost or stolen.

However, you should be aware of the fees and charges that the card provider may apply, such as activation fees, loading fees, withdrawal fees, or inactivity fees. You should also check the balance and validity of your card regularly, as some cards may expire or lose value over time.

Tipping and Service Charges

Tipping in Crete is not obligatory, but it is customary and appreciated for good service or kindness. The amount of the tip depends on your satisfaction and discretion, but below are some general guidelines:

Restaurants and Bars: A service charge of 10% to 15% is usually included in the bill, but you can leave an extra tip of 5% to 10% if you are happy with the service and the food. You can either round up the bill or leave the tip on the table or in the tip jar. If there is no service charge, you can tip 10% to 20% of the bill. You can also tip the waiter or waitress directly, rather than leaving it on the table, to ensure that they receive it.

Hotels: A service charge of 10% to 15% is usually included in the bill, but you can leave an extra tip of €1 to €2 per night for the housekeeping staff, and €1 to €2 per bag for the porter. You can also tip the concierge, the room service, or the valet, depending on the level of service and the type of hotel.

Taxis: A service charge of 10% to 15% is usually included in the meter, but you can round up the fare or leave an extra tip of 5% to 10% if you are satisfied with the driver and the ride. You can also tip more for longer trips or special services, such as tours or transfers.

Guides and Drivers: You can tip your guide or driver 10% to 20% of the total cost of the tour or transfer, depending on the quality and duration of the service. You can also tip more for exceptional service or extra assistance.

Other Services: You can tip other service providers, such as hairdressers, masseurs, or beauticians, 10% to 15% of the total cost of the service, depending on your satisfaction and discretion. You can also tip more for special treatments or extra care.

Accommodation Options

Crete offers a wide range of accommodation options for every taste, budget, and occasion. Whether you are looking for a luxurious resort, a cozy hotel, a charming villa, a traditional guesthouse, or a unique experience, you will find it on this beautiful and diverse island. Below are some of the most common and popular accommodation options in Crete:

Resorts: If you want to enjoy the ultimate comfort, service, and facilities, you can choose from the many resorts that are scattered along the coast of Crete. Resorts are ideal for families, couples, or groups who want to have everything at their fingertips, such as pools, spas, restaurants, bars, entertainment, sports, and activities. Resorts also offer access to some of the best beaches on the island, as well as stunning views of the sea or the mountains. Some of the most famous resorts in Crete are Out of the Blue Resort & Spa, Lyttos Mare, and Elounda Beach Hotel & Villas.

Hotels: If you prefer a more affordable and flexible option, you can opt for one of the many hotels that are available in the main towns and villages of Crete. Hotels are suitable for solo travelers, couples, or friends who want to explore the island and its attractions, as well as enjoy the local culture and cuisine. Hotels range from budget to luxury, and from modern to traditional, depending on your preferences and needs. Some of the most recommended hotels in Crete are Casa Delfino Hotel & Spa, Kydon The Heart City Hotel, and White Swan.

Villas: If you are looking for a more private and

spacious option, you can rent one of the many villas that are located in the countryside or near the beach of Crete. Villas are perfect for families, groups, or couples who want to have their own home away from home, with all the amenities and comforts, such as kitchen, living room, garden, and pool. Villas also offer the opportunity to experience the authentic and traditional Cretan lifestyle, as well as the natural beauty and tranquility of the island. Some of the most popular villas in Crete are Villa Kerasia, Villa Ippocampi, and Villa Athermigo.

Guesthouses: If you are looking for a more cozy and friendly option, you can stay in one of the many guesthouses that are situated in the historic centers or the rural areas of Crete. Guesthouses are ideal for travelers who want to mingle with the locals and learn more about their culture and customs, as well as enjoy the hospitality and the homemade food. Guesthouses are usually family-run and offer simple but comfortable rooms, with shared or private bathrooms, and sometimes a common kitchen or lounge. Some of the most charming guesthouses in Crete are Veneto Boutique Hotel, Kapsaliana Village Hotel, and Metohi Georgila.

Unique Experiences: If you are looking for a more

adventurous and memorable option, you can try one of the many unique experiences that are offered in Crete. These include staying in a historic building, such as a Venetian mansion, a Turkish house, or a Byzantine monastery, that have been restored and converted into accommodation. You can also stay in an agritourism property, such as a farm, a winery, or an olive mill, that produce and sell their own products, and offer activities and workshops. You can also stay in a cave, a treehouse, or a yurt, that provide a different and exciting way to connect with nature. Some of the most amazing unique experiences in Crete are Domus Renier Boutique Hotel, Dalabelos Estate, and Matala Caves.

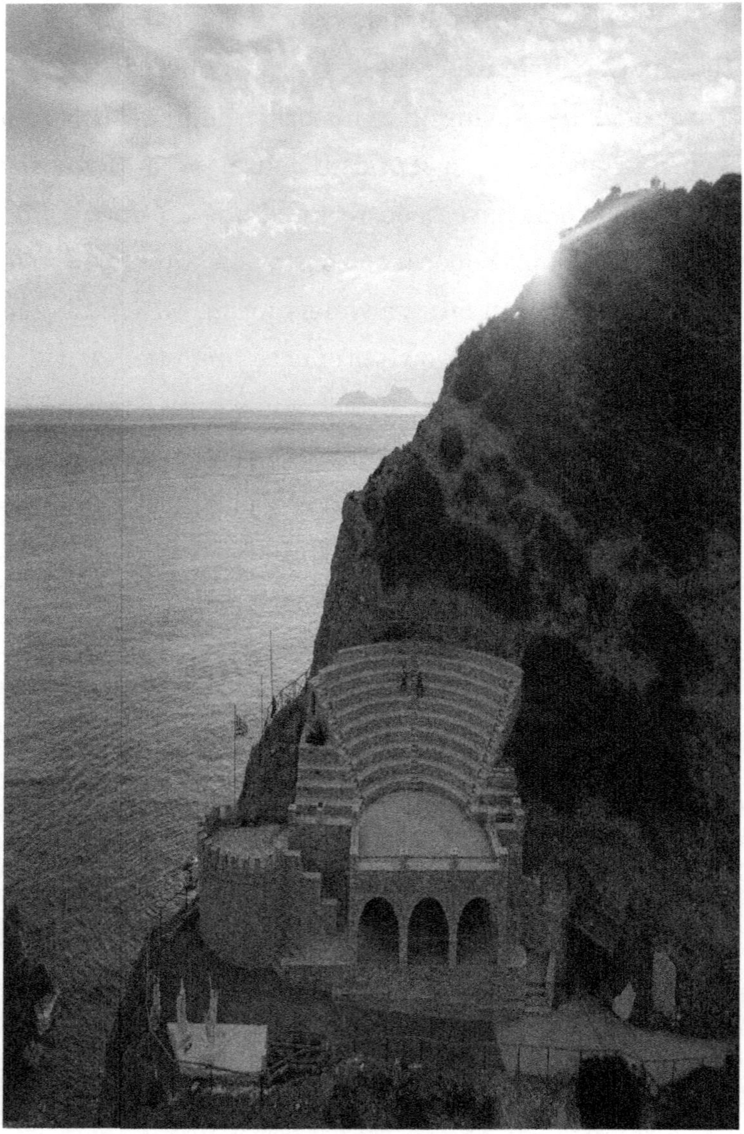

Chapter 3 • Cretan Culture and Etiquette

Cretan Language and Basic Phrases

Crete is part of Greece, and therefore, the official language is Greek. Greek is a Indo-European language, with a rich and ancient history, and a distinctive alphabet. Greek has many dialects, and the one spoken in Crete is known as Cretan or Cretan Greek. Cretan has some differences from standard Greek, in terms of pronunciation, vocabulary, and grammar, but it is mutually intelligible with it. Cretan is also influenced by other languages, such as Venetian, Turkish, and Arabic, due to the island's history and geography.

Most Cretans can speak and understand standard Greek, as well as English, especially in the tourist areas. However, learning some basic phrases and words in Greek and Cretan can help you communicate better with the locals, and show your respect and appreciation for their culture and hospitality. Below are some of the most useful and common phrases and words to know before

35

traveling to Crete:

Greetings and Farewells

Hello: Γεια σας (Yia sas) or Γεια σου (Yia sou) - The first one is more formal and plural, while the second one is more informal and singular. You can use them at any time of the day, as a greeting or a farewell.

Good morning: Καλημέρα (Kalimera) - You can use it until noon, as a greeting or a farewell.

Good afternoon: Καλησπέρα (Kalispera) - You can use it from noon until sunset, as a greeting or a farewell.

Good evening: Καληνύχτα (Kalinikhta) - You can use it after sunset, as a farewell only.

Goodbye: Αντίο (Antio) - You can use it when leaving, as a farewell only.

Polite Expressions

Please: Παρακαλώ (Parakalo) - You can use it to ask for something, to offer something, or to accept something.

Thank you: Ευχαριστώ (Efharisto) - You can use it to express gratitude or appreciation.

You're welcome: Παρακαλώ (Parakalo) - You can use it to respond to thank you, or to mean don't mention it or it's nothing.

Excuse me: Με συγχωρείτε (Me sighoreite) or Συγγνώμη (Singnomi) - You can use the first one to get someone's

36

attention, or to apologize for something, and the second one to get past someone, or to express regret or sorrow.

I'm sorry: Λυπάμαι (Lipame) - You can use it to express sympathy or remorse.

Basic Questions and Answers

How are you?: Τι κάνετε; (Ti kanete?) or Τι κάνεις; (Ti kanis?) - The first one is more formal and plural, while the second one is more informal and singular. You can use them to ask about someone's well-being or mood.

I'm fine, and you?: Καλά, εσείς; (Kala, esis?) or Καλά, εσύ; (Kala, esi?) - The first one is more formal and plural, while the second one is more informal and singular. You can use them to answer the previous question, and to ask back.

What is your name?: Πώς σας λένε; (Pos sas lene?) or Πώς σε λένε; (Pos se lene?) - The first one is more formal and plural, while the second one is more informal and singular. You can use them to ask about someone's name.

My name is...: Με λένε... (Me lene...) - You can use it to introduce yourself or to answer the previous question.

Where are you from?: Από πού είστε; (Apo pou iste?) or Από πού είσαι; (Apo pou ise?) - The first one is more formal and plural, while the second one is more informal and singular. You can use them to ask about someone's origin or nationality.

I'm from...: Είμαι από... (Ime apo...) - You can use it to answer the previous question, or to state your origin or nationality.

Do you speak English?: Μιλάτε αγγλικά; (Milate anglika?) or Μιλάς αγγλικά; (Milas anglika?) - The first one is more formal and plural, while the second one is more informal and singular. You can use them to ask about someone's language skills or to start a conversation.

Yes: Ναι (Ne) - You can use it to answer affirmatively or to agree with something.

No: Όχι (Ohi) - You can use it to answer negatively or to disagree with something.

Numbers and Time

Zero: Μηδέν (Miden)

One: Ένα (Ena)

Two: Δύο (Dio)

Three: Τρία (Tria)

Four: Τέσσερα (Tessera)

Five: Πέντε (Pente)

Six: Έξι (Exi)

Seven: Επτά (Epta)

Eight: Οκτώ (Okto)

Nine: Εννιά (Ennia)

Ten: Δέκα (Deka)

Eleven: Έντεκα (Enteka)

Twelve: Δώδεκα (Dodeka)

Thirteen: Δεκατρία (Dekatria)

Fourteen: Δεκατέσσερα (Dekatessera)

Fifteen: Δεκαπέντε (Dekapente)

Sixteen: Δεκαέξι (Dekaexi)

Seventeen: Δεκαεπτά (Dekaepta)

Eighteen: Δεκαοκτώ (Dekaokto)

Nineteen: Δεκαεννιά (Dekaennia)

Twenty: Είκοσι (Ikosi)

Twenty-one: Είκοσι ένα (Ikosi ena)

Twenty-two: Είκοσι δύο (Ikosi dio)

Thirty: Τριάντα (Trianta)

Forty: Σαράντα (Saranta)

Fifty: Πενήντα (Peninta)

Sixty: Εξήντα (Exinta)

Seventy: Εβδομήντα (Evdominta)

Eighty: Ογδόντα (Ogdon

Cultural Norms and Customs

Cretans are known for their hospitality, pride, and

rebelliousness, as well as their love for life, food, and music. Crete is a place where you can experience the authentic and traditional Cretan lifestyle, as well as the modern and cosmopolitan aspects of the island. Below are some of the most important and interesting cultural norms and customs to know before traveling to Crete:

Family and Community: Cretans value family and community above all, and they often live in extended families or close-knit neighborhoods. They respect their elders and ancestors, and they celebrate their name days and saints' days with great fervor. They also have a strong sense of solidarity and mutual aid, especially in times of need or crisis. Cretans are friendly and welcoming to visitors, and they often invite them to share a meal, a drink, or a conversation. They also expect visitors to respect their culture and traditions, and to behave politely and modestly.

Religion and Festivals: Cretans are mostly Orthodox Christians, and religion plays a significant role in their culture and identity. They have many churches and monasteries, some of which date back to the Byzantine era, and they often display religious icons and symbols in their homes and cars. They observe the religious holidays and rituals, such as Easter, Christmas, and

Lent, with devotion and enthusiasm. They also have many local festivals and celebrations, known as panigiria, which usually involve music, dance, food, and drink. Some of the most popular panigiria are the Feast of the Assumption of the Virgin Mary on August 15th, the Feast of Saint John the Baptist on June 24th, and the Feast of Saint George on April 23rd.

Food and Drink: Cretans are famous for their cuisine, which is based on the Mediterranean diet and the local produce. They use olive oil, cheese, honey, herbs, vegetables, fruits, fish, and meat, to create simple but delicious dishes, such as dakos, kalitsounia, snails, gamopilafo, and raki. They also have a variety of pastries and sweets, such as kalitsounia, xerotigana, and loukoumades. Cretans enjoy eating and drinking in good company, and they often gather around a table or a taverna, to share their food, stories, and jokes. They also offer food and drink to their guests, as a sign of hospitality and generosity.

Music and Dance: Cretans have a rich musical and dance heritage, which expresses their emotions, history, and identity. They use traditional instruments, such as the lyra, the lute, the mandolin, and the tambourine, to create melodies and rhythms that are unique and captivating. They also sing songs, known as mantinades, which are improvised verses that convey messages of love, sorrow, humor, or wisdom. Cretans love to dance, and they have many dances, such as the pentozali, the syrtos, the maleviziotis, and the sousta, that are performed in circles, lines, or pairs. Cretans dance at weddings, festivals, or any occasion, to celebrate life and to express their spirit and character.

Dress and Appearance: Cretans have a distinctive dress and appearance, that reflects their origin and personality. They wear traditional costumes, especially on special occasions, such as weddings, festivals, or parades. The men's costume consists of a black shirt, a black breeches, a black sash, a black cap, and black boots. The women's costume consists of a white blouse, a colorful skirt, a colorful apron, a colorful scarf, and colorful shoes. Cretans also wear jewelry and accessories, such as rings, earrings, necklaces, and bracelets, that are made of gold, silver, or other materials. Cretans take pride in their appearance, and they often dress elegantly and stylishly, even in casual settings.

Dining Etiquette

Below are some of the most important and common dining etiquette tips to know before traveling to Crete:

When you are invited to a Cretan home for a meal, you should not be punctual, as it is considered rude and impatient. You should arrive about 30 minutes late, and bring a small gift, such as flowers, cakes, or wine. You should also compliment the host on their food and hospitality, and offer to help with the dishes or the cleaning.

When you are dining at a taverna or a restaurant, you should not expect a menu, as most places serve what is available and fresh. You can ask the waiter or the owner for suggestions, or look at what other people are eating. You should also not expect separate plates or courses, as most dishes are shared among the table. You can use your bread to dip into the sauces or the olive oil, but do not leave any crumbs on the table or the floor.

When you are paying for your meal, you should not tip too much, as it is not customary or expected in Crete. A service charge of 10% to 15% is usually included in the bill, but you can leave an extra tip of 5% to 10% if you are happy with the service and the food. You can either round up the bill or leave the tip on the table or in the tip jar. If there is no service charge, you can tip 10% to 20% of the bill. You can also tip the waiter or waitress directly, rather than leaving it on the table, to ensure that they receive it.

When you are drinking raki, the traditional alcoholic drink made from grapes, you should not drink it all at once, as it is very strong and can make you drunk quickly. You should sip it slowly, and accompany it with water, meze, or fruits. You should also not refuse a glass of raki, as it is considered rude and offensive. You should accept it with a smile, and say "yamas", which means cheers. You should also not mix raki with other drinks, such as beer or wine, as it is considered disrespectful and wasteful.

Dress Code and Fashion in Crete

Below are some tips and suggestions to help you pack and dress appropriately for your trip to Crete:

General Tips: Crete is a casual and relaxed destination, where you can wear whatever you feel comfortable and confident in. However, there are some general tips that you should keep in mind, such as:

Choose light, breathable, and natural fabrics, such as

cotton, linen, or silk, to cope with the warm and sunny weather, especially in the summer months. Avoid synthetic, dark, or heavy fabrics, such as polyester, wool, or leather, that may cause you to sweat or overheat.

Pack layers, such as cardigans, jackets, or scarves, to adjust to the temperature changes, especially in the spring and fall seasons. Crete can be windy and chilly at night, or in the mountains, so it is good to have something to cover up with.

Bring comfortable and sturdy shoes, such as sneakers, sandals, or hiking boots, to walk on the uneven and rocky terrain, or to explore the gorges, the mountains, or the countryside. Avoid high heels, flip flops, or bare feet, that may cause you to slip, trip, or injure yourself.

Wear sunscreen, sunglasses, and hats, to protect yourself from the sun, which can be very strong and harmful, especially in the summer months. Crete has a high UV index, so it is important to apply sunscreen regularly and avoid sunburns.

Respect the local culture and customs, especially when visiting religious or historical sites, such as churches, monasteries, or museums. Avoid wearing clothes that are too short, tight, or revealing, such as shorts, skirts, tank tops, or bikinis, that may be considered inappropriate or offensive. Opt for clothes that cover your shoulders, knees, and chest, such as pants, dresses, or shirts, that may be more respectful and modest.

What to Wear in Crete in Summer (June, July, and August): Summer is the peak season in Crete, when the island is full of tourists and the weather is hot and dry. The average temperature ranges from 23°C (73°F) to 29°C (84°F), and the sea temperature is around 26°C (79°F). The summer is the best time to enjoy the beach, the sea, and the sun, but also to experience the nightlife, the festivals, and the events. Below are some examples of what to wear in Crete in summer:

For the beach: You can wear your swimsuit, bikini, or trunks, to swim, sunbathe, or relax on the beach. You can also wear a cover-up, such as a kaftan, a sarong, or a dress, to go to the beach bar, the taverna, or the shop. You can also wear flip flops, sandals, or water shoes, to walk on the sand, the pebbles, or the rocks. You can also wear a sun hat, sunglasses, and sunscreen, to protect yourself from the sun. You can also bring a beach bag, a towel, a book, or a game, to enjoy your time on the beach. Some of the most popular beaches in Crete are Elafonisi, Balos, Vai, and Preveli.

46

For the town: You can wear light, airy, and colorful clothes, such as shorts, skirts, dresses, or pants, to walk around the town, visit the attractions, or do some shopping. You can also wear tank tops, T-shirts, blouses, or shirts, to match your bottoms, or to layer over your swimsuit. You can also wear sneakers, sandals, or flats, to walk comfortably and stylishly on the streets, the alleys, or the squares. You can also wear a hat, sunglasses, and sunscreen, to protect yourself from the sun. You can also bring a backpack, a tote, or a crossbody bag, to carry your essentials, such as your wallet, your phone, your camera, or your water bottle. Some of the most charming towns in Crete are Chania, Rethymno, Heraklion, and Agios Nikolaos.

For the night: You can wear chic, elegant, and glamorous clothes, such as dresses, skirts, pants, or jumpsuits, to go out for dinner, drinks, or dancing. You can also wear tops, jackets, or accessories, such as jewelry, scarves, or belts, to add some flair and sparkle to your outfit. You can also wear heels, wedges, or boots, to elevate your look and your height. You can also wear a shawl, a cardigan, or a coat, to keep you warm and cozy in the cooler nights. You can also bring a clutch, a purse, or a wallet, to hold your money, your cards, or your keys.

Some of the most lively and fun places in Crete are Malia, Hersonissos, Platanias, and Agia Marina.

What to Wear in Crete in Spring (March, April, and May) and Fall (September, October, and November): Spring and fall are the shoulder seasons in Crete, when the island is less crowded and the weather is mild and pleasant. The average temperature ranges from 15°C (59°F) to 23°C (73°F), and the sea temperature is around 20°C (68°F). The spring and fall are the best time to enjoy the nature, the culture, and the activities, but also to experience the festivals, the events, and the traditions. Below are some examples of what to wear in Crete in spring and fall:

For hiking: You can wear comfortable, durable, and versatile clothes, such as pants, leggings, shorts, or skirts, to hike on the trails, the gorges, or the mountains. You can also wear tops, sweaters, hoodies, or jackets, to layer according to the temperature and the altitude. You can also wear hiking boots, sneakers, or sandals, to walk on the uneven and rocky terrain. You can also wear a hat, sunglasses, and sunscreen, to protect yourself from the sun. You can also bring a backpack, a water bottle, a snack, or a map, to enjoy your hike. Some of the most amazing hiking spots in Crete are Samaria Gorge,

Imbros Gorge, Psiloritis Mountain, and Lassithi Plateau.

For sightseeing: You can wear casual, smart, and modest clothes, such as pants, dresses, skirts, or jumpsuits, to visit the historical, archaeological, or religious sites. You can also wear tops, shirts, blouses, or cardigans, to match your bottoms, or to cover your shoulders and chest. You can also wear flats, sandals, or sneakers, to walk comfortably and respectfully on the sites. You can also wear a hat, sunglasses, and sunscreen, to protect yourself from the sun. You can also bring a tote, a crossbody, or a backpack, to carry your essentials, such as your wallet, your phone, your camera, or your guidebook. Some of the most impressive sites in Crete are Knossos Palace, Phaistos Palace, Arkadi Monastery, and Spinalonga Island.

For dining: You can wear stylish, sophisticated, and cozy clothes, such as pants, skirts, dresses, or jumpsuits, to enjoy the delicious Cretan cuisine and wine. You can also wear tops, jackets, coats, or accessories, such as jewelry, scarves, or hats, to add some warmth and charm to your outfit. You can also wear heels, wedges, or flats, to complete your look and your mood. You can also bring a purse, a clutch, or a wallet, to hold your money, your cards, or your keys. Some of the most popular dishes in Crete are dakos, kalitsounia, snails, gamopilafo, and raki.

Festivals and Celebrations

Below are some of the most popular and interesting festivals and celebrations that you should not miss when you visit Crete:

Easter: Easter is the most important and festive occasion in Crete, as well as in the rest of Greece. It is a time of spiritual reflection, family reunion, and joyful celebration. The Easter festivities begin 40 days before Easter Sunday, with the Lent period, during which people fast from meat, dairy, and other animal products. The Holy Week, the week before Easter, is marked by various rituals and services, such as the Palm Sunday procession, the Holy Thursday mass, the Good Friday epitaphios, and the Holy Saturday resurrection. On Easter Sunday, people gather to feast on lamb, eggs, cheese pies, and other delicacies, and to exchange greetings of "Christos Anesti" (Christ is risen). Easter in Crete is a unique and memorable experience, especially in the villages, where you can witness the authentic and traditional customs and practices of the locals.

Carnival: Carnival is a fun and colorful event that takes place in February or March, before the Lent period. It is a time of masquerade, music, and entertainment, inspired by the ancient Dionysian festivals and the Venetian influence. There are many carnival celebrations in Crete, but the most famous ones are in Rethymno, Heraklion, and Sitia. In Rethymno, the carnival is the largest and longest in Greece, lasting for three weeks and featuring various events, such as parades, parties, concerts, and contests. In Heraklion, the carnival is known for its satirical and political themes, as well as its spectacular floats and costumes. In Sitia, the carnival is known for its traditional dances and songs, as well as its local delicacies, such as xerotigana and kalitsounia.

Agios Georgios: Agios Georgios (Saint George) is one of the most revered saints in Crete, as well as in the rest of Greece. He is the patron saint of shepherds, farmers, and soldiers, and he is celebrated on April 23rd. On this day, there are many festivals and fairs in honor of Saint George, especially in the rural areas and the mountains, where he is considered the protector of the people and the animals. The most popular festivals are in Asi Gonia in Chania and Plakias in Rethymno, where people gather to pray, dance, eat, and drink, and to seek the blessings of the saint.

Agios Ioannis: Agios Ioannis (Saint John) is another popular saint in Crete, who is celebrated on June 24th. He is also known as Ioannis Prodromos (John the Baptist), and he is the precursor of Christ. On this day, there are many festivals and celebrations in honor of Saint John, especially in the western part of the island, where he is highly cherished. The most famous festival is in Agia Irini in Chania, where people light bonfires and jump over them, following an ancient custom that symbolizes purification and fertility.

Assumption of the Virgin Mary: The Assumption of the Virgin Mary, also known as the Dormition of the Virgin Mary, is the largest religious festival in Crete, as well as in the rest of Greece. It is celebrated on August 15th, and it commemorates the belief that the Virgin Mary, after her death, was taken up into heaven both in body and soul. On this day, almost every village in Crete has a church or a chapel dedicated to the Virgin Mary, and organizes a festival or a fair to honor her. The most famous festivals are in the Monastery of Panagia Chrissoskalitissa in Chania and in the Byzantine church of Panagia Kera in Lassithi.

Houdetsi Festival: Houdetsi Festival is a four-day

celebration of music, food, and art, that takes place in August in the village of Houdetsi, 23 km south of Heraklion. It is organized by Ross Daly, a renowned musician and composer, who founded the Labyrinth Musical Workshop in the village. The festival features local and international artists, who perform various genres and styles of music, such as folk, jazz, classical, and world. The festival also offers workshops, exhibitions, screenings, and other activities, that aim to promote the cultural diversity and the artistic expression of Crete.

Matala Festival: Matala Festival is an international festival that takes place in June in Matala, a seaside village in the south of Heraklion. It is a tribute to the hippie era of the 1960s and 1970s, when Matala was a popular destination for hippies from all over the world, who lived in the caves on the beach. The festival features music, art, and literature from that period, as well as contemporary artists and performers, who share the same spirit and values. The festival also offers camping, yoga, meditation, and other activities, that create a sense of community and harmony.

Wine Festival: Wine Festival is a common event that takes place in many villages in Crete, especially in the summer months. It is a celebration of the wine production and consumption, which is an integral part of the Cretan culture and diet. The wine festival offers free wine tasting, as well as local food, music, and dance, that create a festive and joyful atmosphere. The most famous wine festival is in Anogia, a mountainous village in Rethymno, where the wine is accompanied by cheese, honey, and meat, and the music is played by the legendary lyra player Psarantonis.

Chapter 4 • Exploring Crete

Chania

Chania is a charming city on the northwest coast of Crete, the largest and most populous of the Greek islands. It is the capital of the Chania regional unit, which covers the western part of the island. Chania has a rich and diverse history, culture, and natural beauty, that make it one of the most popular and attractive destinations in Greece.

Chania was the site of the ancient Minoan city of Kydonia, which was later conquered by the Romans, the Byzantines, the Venetians, and the Ottomans. Each of these civilizations left their mark on the city, creating a unique and fascinating blend of architectural styles and influences. The most prominent feature of Chania is its picturesque old town, which is built around the Venetian harbor and the lighthouse. The old town is full of narrow alleys, colorful houses, elegant mansions, and historic monuments, such as the Küçük Hasan mosque, the Grand Arsenal, the Splanzia ruins, and the Byzantine walls. The old town is also home to many museums, churches, and shops, that showcase the art, culture, and traditions of Chania and Crete.

Chania is not only a city of history, but also a city of life. It has a vibrant and cosmopolitan atmosphere, with many cafes, bars, restaurants, and clubs, that cater to all tastes and preferences. Chania is also famous for its cuisine, which is based on the Mediterranean diet and the local produce. You can enjoy the delicious dishes, such as dakos, kalitsounia, snails, gamopilafo, and raki, in the tavernas, the rakadika, or the historic cafes, that offer a feast of flavors and aromas. You can also experience the lively music, the colorful dances, and the festive celebrations, that express the spirit and the soul of Chania and Crete.

Chania is also a city of nature, surrounded by stunning landscapes and scenery. It is located at the end of the homonymous gulf, between the Akrotiri and Onicha peninsulas, and has a mild and pleasant climate. It has many beautiful beaches, such as Agia Marina, Stalos, Platanias, and Nea Chora, where you can swim, sunbathe, or relax. It also has many natural wonders, such as the Samaria Gorge, the Balos Lagoon, and the Elafonisi Beach, where you can hike, explore, or admire. It also has many charming villages, such as Vamos,

Kefalas, Gavalohori, and Agios Pavlos, where you can discover the authentic and traditional Cretan lifestyle.

Chania is a city that will captivate you with its beauty, diversity, and hospitality. It is a city that will offer you an array of unforgettable adventures and experiences, that will make you fall in love with it and Crete.

Rethymno

Rethymno is a beautiful city on the north coast of Crete, the largest and most populous of the Greek islands. It is the capital of the Rethymno regional unit, which covers the central part of the island. Rethymno has a rich and diverse history, culture, and natural beauty, that make it one of the most attractive and charming destinations in Greece.

Rethymno was founded by the ancient Minoans, who ruled the island from the 27th to the 15th century BC. It was later occupied by the Romans, the Byzantines, the Arabs, the Venetians, and the Ottomans, who left their mark on the city's architecture and heritage. The most prominent feature of Rethymno is its old town, which is one of the best-preserved Venetian towns in the Mediterranean. The old town is full of narrow streets, colorful buildings, elegant mansions, and historic monuments, such as the Fortezza, the Rimondi Fountain, the Neratze Mosque, and the Loggia. The old town is also home to many museums, churches, and shops, that showcase the art, culture, and traditions of Rethymno and Crete.

Rethymno is not only a city of history, but also a city of life. It has a vibrant and cosmopolitan atmosphere, with many cafes, bars, restaurants, and clubs, that cater to all tastes and preferences. Rethymno is also famous for its cuisine, which is based on the Mediterranean diet and the local produce. You can enjoy the delicious dishes, such as dakos, kalitsounia, snails, gamopilafo, and raki, in the tavernas, the rakadika, or the kafenia, that offer a feast of flavors and aromas. You can also experience the lively music, the colorful dances, and the festive celebrations, that express the spirit and the soul of Rethymno and Crete.

Rethymno is also a city of nature, surrounded by stunning landscapes and scenery. It is located between the Psiloritis and the White Mountains, and has a mild and pleasant climate. It has many beautiful beaches, such as Adelianos Kampos, Platanes, Perivolia, and Skaleta, where you can swim, sunbathe, or relax. It also has many natural wonders, such as the Kourtaliotiko

Gorge, the Preveli Palm Beach, and the Potami Dam, where you can hike, explore, or admire. It also has many charming villages, such as Anogia, Margarites, Argyroupoli, and Spili, where you can discover the authentic and traditional Cretan lifestyle.

Heraklion

Heraklion is the largest and most populous city on the island of Crete, and the capital of the Heraklion regional unit, which covers the eastern part of the island. Heraklion is a modern and dynamic city, with a rich and diverse history, culture, and natural beauty, that make it one of the most attractive and interesting destinations in Greece.

Heraklion was the center of the Minoan civilization, the oldest and most advanced civilization in Europe, which flourished from the 27th to the 15th century BC. The city is home to the famous palace of Knossos, the largest and most complex of the Minoan palaces, which is considered the oldest city in Europe. The palace is a must-see attraction, as it reveals the splendor and the mystery of the Minoan culture, with its colorful frescoes, intricate architecture, and sophisticated technology. The palace is also connected to the legends of King Minos, the Minotaur, and the Labyrinth, which have inspired many artists and writers throughout history.

Heraklion was also influenced by other civilizations and cultures, such as the Romans, the Byzantines, the Arabs, the Venetians, and the Ottomans, who left their mark on the city's architecture and heritage. The most prominent feature of Heraklion is its Venetian fortress, known as Koules or Castello, which dominates the harbor and the seafront. The fortress was built in the 16th century, and it served as a defense and a prison, as well as a symbol of the Venetian power and glory. The fortress is open to the public, and it offers stunning views of the city and the sea, as well as a museum and a cultural venue.

Heraklion is not only a city of history, but also a city of life. It has a vibrant and cosmopolitan atmosphere, with many cafes, bars, restaurants, and clubs, that cater to all tastes and preferences. Heraklion is also famous for its cuisine, which is based on the Mediterranean diet and the local produce. You can enjoy the delicious dishes, such as dakos, kalitsounia, snails, gamopilafo, and raki, in the tavernas, the rakadika, or the historic cafes, that offer a feast of flavors and aromas. You can also experience the lively music, the colorful dances, and the festive celebrations, that express the spirit and the soul of Heraklion and Crete

Heraklion is also a city of nature, surrounded by stunning landscapes and scenery. It is located on the north coast of Crete, and it has a mild and pleasant climate. It has many beautiful beaches, such as Amoudara, Karteros, Kokkini Hani, and Agia Pelagia, where you can swim, sunbathe, or relax. It also has many natural wonders, such as the Cave of Zeus, the birthplace of the king of the gods, according to the Greek mythology, which is located on the slopes of Mount Ida, the highest mountain in Crete. The cave is a sacred and awe-inspiring site, with stalactites, stalagmites, and an underground lake, that create a magical atmosphere.

Lasithi

Lasithi is the easternmost and least populated regional unit on the island of Crete, to the east of Heraklion. Its capital is Agios Nikolaos, the other major towns being Ierapetra, Sitia, and Neapoli. Lasithi has a diverse and beautiful landscape, ranging from sandy beaches and rocky coves to fertile plains and rugged mountains. Lasithi is also home to some of the most remarkable natural and cultural attractions in Crete, such as the Lasithi Plateau, the palm forest of Vai, and the island of

Spinalonga

Lasithi has a long and rich history, dating back to the Minoan civilization, which flourished on the island from the 27th to the 15th century BC. Lasithi was the site of the ancient Minoan town of Zakros, which was the fourth largest and most important Minoan palace, after Knossos, Phaistos, and Malia. Zakros was a major trade center, connecting Crete with the Near East, Africa, and Egypt. The palace and the surrounding settlement were destroyed by a volcanic eruption around 1450 BC, and remained buried until the 20th century, when they were excavated by the British archaeologist Arthur Evans.

Lasithi was also influenced by other civilizations and cultures, such as the Dorians, the Romans, the Byzantines, the Arabs, the Venetians, and the Ottomans, who left their mark on the region's architecture and heritage. The most prominent feature of Lasithi is the Lasithi Plateau, a high endorheic plateau, located in the Dikti Mountains, at an average altitude of 840 m (2,760 ft). The plateau is famous for its white-sailed windmills, which were used since the 1920s to irrigate the land. The plateau is also the birthplace of Zeus, the king of the gods, according to the Greek mythology. The Cave of Zeus, where he was born and raised by the nymphs, is a sacred and awe-inspiring site, with stalactites, stalagmites, and an underground lake.

Lasithi is not only a region of history, but also a region of life. It has a vibrant and cosmopolitan atmosphere, with many cafes, bars, restaurants, and clubs, that cater to all tastes and preferences. Lasithi is also famous for its cuisine, which is based on the Mediterranean diet and the local produce. You can enjoy the delicious dishes, such as dakos, kalitsounia, snails, gamopilafo, and raki, in the tavernas, the rakadika, or the kafenia, that offer a feast of flavors and aromas. You can also experience the lively music, the colorful dances, and the festive celebrations, that express the spirit and the soul of Lasithi and Crete.

Lasithi is also a region of nature, surrounded by stunning landscapes and scenery. It has many beautiful beaches, such as Vai, Agia Fotia, Makrigialos, and Xerokambos, where you can swim, sunbathe, or relax. Vai is especially famous for its palm forest, the largest in Europe, which creates a tropical and exotic setting. Lasithi also has many natural wonders, such as the Richtis Gorge, the Chrysopigi Monastery, and the Toplou Monastery, where you can hike, explore, or admire. Lasithi also has many charming islands, such as

Spinalonga, Chrissi, and Koufonisi, where you can discover the history, the culture, and the beauty of the region.

Chapter 5 • Top Attractions

The Palace of Knossos

The Palace of Knossos is one of the most famous and impressive archaeological sites in Crete, and in the world. It is the largest and most complex of the Minoan palaces, the ancient civilization that flourished on the island from the 27th to the 15th century BC. The palace is located on the outskirts of Heraklion, the capital of Crete, and covers an area of about 14,000 square meters. The palace was the political, economic, and religious center of the Minoan civilization, and the residence of the legendary King Minos, who ruled over Crete and the Aegean Sea. According to the Greek mythology, the palace was also the home of the Minotaur, a half-man half-bull creature that was kept in a labyrinth and fed with human sacrifices. The palace was also connected to the myths of Theseus, the hero who killed the Minotaur, Daedalus, the inventor who built the labyrinth, and Icarus, his son who flew too close to the sun.

The palace was built around 1900 BC, on the site of an older settlement that dated back to the Neolithic period.

The palace was destroyed and rebuilt several times, due to earthquakes, fires, or invasions, until its final abandonment around 1350 BC. The palace had four main wings, arranged around a central court, and consisted of hundreds of rooms, such as storerooms, workshops, shrines, throne rooms, banquet halls, and living quarters. The palace was decorated with colorful frescoes, depicting scenes from nature, religion, sports, and everyday life. The palace also had advanced features, such as drainage systems, water supply, ventilation, and lighting.

The palace was rediscovered in 1878 by Minos Kalokairinos, a Cretan merchant and antiquarian, who excavated part of the storerooms. In 1900, Arthur Evans, a British archaeologist and scholar, started a more extensive and systematic excavation, which lasted until 1931. Evans unearthed most of the palace, as well as many artifacts, such as pottery, jewelry, tools, weapons, and the famous Linear B tablets, the earliest form of Greek writing. Evans also restored and reconstructed parts of the palace, using concrete, wood, and paint, to give an idea of how it looked like in its original state. However, his work is controversial, as some of his interventions are considered inaccurate, irreversible, or intrusive.

The palace is open to the public, and it is one of the most visited attractions in Crete. Visitors can explore the palace and its surroundings, and admire the architecture, the art, and the culture of the Minoans. Visitors can also learn more about the history, the mythology, and the mysteries of the palace, through guided tours, audio guides, or signs. The palace is also a cultural venue, hosting various events, such as concerts, exhibitions, and festivals.

Agios Nikolaos

Agios Nikolaos is a picturesque city on the eastern coast of Crete, the largest and most populous of the Greek islands. It is the capital of the Lasithi regional unit, which covers the eastern part of the island. Agios Nikolaos has a rich and diverse history, culture, and natural beauty, that make it one of the most attractive and charming destinations in Greece.

Agios Nikolaos was founded by the ancient Minoans, who ruled the island from the 27th to the 15th century BC. It was later occupied by the Romans, the Byzantines, the Arabs, the Venetians, and the Ottomans, who left their mark on the city's architecture and heritage. The name Agios Nikolaos means Saint Nicholas, the patron saint of sailors and of all of Greece. The most prominent feature of Agios Nikolaos is its small lagoon, known as Lake Voulismeni, which is connected to the sea by a narrow canal. The lake is surrounded by cafes, restaurants, and shops, and it offers a scenic and romantic setting. The lake is also the site of a legend, according to which the goddess Athena bathed in its waters.

Agios Nikolaos is not only a city of history, but also a city of life. It has a vibrant and cosmopolitan atmosphere, with many cafes, bars, restaurants, and clubs, that cater to all tastes and preferences. Agios Nikolaos is also famous for its cuisine, which is based on the Mediterranean diet and the local produce. You can enjoy the delicious dishes, such as dakos, kalitsounia, snails, gamopilafo, and raki, in the tavernas, the rakadika, or the historic cafes, that offer a feast of flavors and aromas. You can also experience the lively music, the colorful dances, and the festive celebrations, that express the spirit and the soul of Agios Nikolaos and Crete.

Agios Nikolaos is also a city of nature, surrounded by stunning landscapes and scenery. It is located on the

Mirabello Bay, which is the largest bay in Crete, and it has a mild and pleasant climate. It has many beautiful beaches, such as Almyros, Ammoudi, Kitroplatia, and Ammoudara, where you can swim, sunbathe, or relax. It also has many natural wonders, such as the island of Agioi Pantes, which is a small rocky island with a chapel and a lighthouse, and the island of Spinalonga, which is a former leper colony and a fortress, and a popular tourist attraction.

Samaria Gorge

Samaria Gorge is one of the most spectacular and popular natural attractions in Crete, and in Greece. It is a 16 km long national park, located in the southwest of the island, in the regional unit of Chania. It is the longest and deepest gorge in Europe, and a World's Biosphere Reserve.

Samaria Gorge was formed by a small river that carved its way through the White Mountains, creating a stunning landscape of cliffs, rocks, and forests. The gorge is home to a rich and diverse flora and fauna, with over 450 species of plants and animals, many of which are endemic to Crete. The most famous inhabitant of the gorge is the kri-kri, the Cretan wild goat, which is endangered and protected by the park.

The gorge is open to visitors from May to October, and it offers a unique and challenging hiking experience. The hike starts at an altitude of 1,250 m, at the northern entrance of the park, near the village of Omalos. The hike ends at the southern exit of the park, at the coastal village of Agia Roumeli, on the Libyan Sea. The hike takes about five to seven hours, depending on the pace and the fitness level of the hikers. The hike is not suitable for children under six years old, people with health problems, or people with fear of heights.

The hike is rewarding and unforgettable, as it passes through various landscapes and sceneries, such as forests, meadows, streams, and springs. The most famous part of the hike is the stretch known as the Gates, or the Iron Gates, where the gorge narrows to a width of only four meters, and the walls rise up to 300 meters. The hike also passes through the abandoned village of Samaria, which was once inhabited by about 500 people, who lived off farming and logging. The village was evacuated in 1962, when the gorge became a national park. The village takes its name from the ancient church of Osia Maria, which stands in the center of the village.

The hike ends at Agia Roumeli, a small and picturesque village, where hikers can rest, eat, and swim. From there, they can take a ferry to the nearby villages of Sougia, Paleochora, or Hora Sfakion, where they can spend the night, or catch a bus back to Chania. Alternatively, they can stay in Agia Roumeli, and enjoy the tranquility and the beauty of the place.

Heraklion Archaeological Museum

If you are interested in the ancient history and culture of Crete, you should not miss the Heraklion Archaeological Museum, one of the largest and most impressive museums in Greece. The museum houses the most important and complete collection of artefacts from the Minoan civilization, the oldest and most advanced civilization in Europe, which flourished on the island from the 27th to the 15th century BC. The museum also displays artefacts from other periods of Cretan history, from the Neolithic to the Roman times, covering a chronological span of over 5,500 years.

The museum is located in the center of Heraklion, the capital of Crete, and it occupies a two-story building that was originally designed as a power station in 1937. The building was severely damaged during the Second World War, and it was restored and converted into a museum in 1952. The museum underwent a major renovation and expansion from 2006 to 2014, which improved its facilities, services, and exhibitions. The museum has 27 galleries, covering a total area of 8,000 square meters, and it can accommodate up to 2,500 visitors per day.

The museum's collection consists of more than 15,000 artefacts, which are arranged in chronological and thematic order, and accompanied by informative labels, maps, and multimedia. The museum's highlights include:

The Minoan collection, which showcases the masterpieces of Minoan art and technology, such as the Phaistos Disc, a clay disc with a mysterious script, the Snake Goddess, a faience figurine of a female deity, the Bull-Leaping Fresco, a wall painting depicting a ritual sport, the Harvester Vase, a stone vase with a relief of a procession of farmers, and the Linear B tablets, the earliest form of Greek writing.

The prehistoric collection, which displays artefacts from the Neolithic and the Early Bronze Age, such as pottery, tools, weapons, jewelry, and figurines, that illustrate the development of the Cretan society and culture before the emergence of the Minoans.

The historical collection, which exhibits artefacts from the Late Bronze Age to the Roman period, such as pottery, sculpture, metalwork, coins, and mosaics, that reflect the influence and interaction of the Cretans with other civilizations, such as the Mycenaeans, the Dorians, the Romans, and the Egyptians.

The temporary exhibitions, which present special topics or themes related to Cretan archaeology and history, such as the Minoan shipbuilding, the Cretan diet, or the Cretan mythology.

The museum also offers various facilities and services to its visitors, such as a gift shop, a cafeteria, a library, a conference hall, and a children's area. The museum also organizes various educational and cultural activities, such as guided tours, workshops, lectures, and concerts. The museum is open daily from 8:00 to 20:00, except on Mondays when it is closed. The entrance fee is 10 euros for adults, 5 euros for students and seniors, and free for children under 18. The museum also offers a combined ticket with the Knossos Palace, the largest and most complex of the Minoan palaces, for 16 euros.

Preveli Monastery and Preveli Beach

Preveli Monastery

Preveli Monastery is a sacred and historical site, located on the south coast of Crete, in the regional unit of Rethymno. It is one of the most famous and beautiful monasteries on the island, overlooking the Libyan Sea and the exotic palm forest of Preveli Beach.

Preveli Monastery consists of two main building complexes, the Lower Monastery of St. John the Baptist, and the Upper Monastery of St. John the Theologian. The Lower Monastery, which is now in ruins, was founded in the 10th or 11th century, and it was the original seat of the monastery. The Upper Monastery, which is still operational, was built in the 17th century, and it is the current seat of the monastery. The Upper Monastery has a fortress-like appearance, with a high wall and a tower, and it contains a church, a museum, a library, and a guesthouse.

Preveli Monastery has played an important role in the history and culture of Crete, as it was involved in many rebellions and wars against the foreign invaders, such as the Venetians, the Ottomans, and the Germans. The monastery was a center of education and art, and it hosted many prominent figures, such as the Cretan painter Ioannis Kornaros, and the Cretan poet Vitsentzos Kornaros, the author of the famous romance "Erotokritos". The monastery also provided shelter and assistance to many Allied soldiers during the Second World War, especially to the Australian and New Zealand troops, who were stranded on the island after the Battle of Crete in 1941. The monastery was destroyed several times by the enemies, but it was always rebuilt and restored by the monks and the locals.

Preveli Monastery is open to the public, and it is a popular tourist attraction, as well as a place of pilgrimage and worship. Visitors can admire the architecture, the art, and the relics of the monastery, as well as the stunning views of the sea and the palm forest. Visitors can also learn more about the history, the mythology, and the mysteries of the monastery, through guided tours, audio guides, or signs. The monastery is also a cultural venue, hosting various events, such as concerts, exhibitions, and festivals.

Preveli Beach

Preveli beach and lagoon (Greek Λίμνη του Πρέβελη), sometimes known locally as "Palm Beach", is located below the monastery, at the mouth of the Kourtaliótiko gorge. Behind the beach is an extensive glade of palm trees. According to a local legend, the King of Ithaca, Odysseus, remained in the wider area of Lake Preveli after the end of the Trojan War, on his return to Ithaca from Troy. The area is a popular tourist destination due to the river, the forest with palm trees in the gorge, and the sandy beach with clear waters. On the beach, there is a rock in the shape of a heart "The stone of lovers" according to the locals.

The beach can be reached by boat from the nearby villages of Plakias or Agia Galini, or by foot from the monastery, following a steep and rocky path. The beach is not organized, so visitors should bring their own supplies, such as water, food, and sunscreen. The beach is also a protected area, so visitors should respect the natural environment, and avoid littering, camping, or lighting fires. The beach is ideal for swimming, snorkeling, or relaxing, but it can be crowded and windy in the summer months.

Matala Beach

Matala Beach is a stunning and historic beach on the south coast of Crete, in the regional unit of Heraklion. It is famous for its natural caves, which were carved into the cliffs by the sea and the wind, and which were used as dwellings, tombs, and places of worship by various civilizations, such as the Minoans, the Romans, and the Byzantines.

Matala Beach is also known for its hippie culture, which flourished in the 1960s and 1970s, when the caves became a refuge for travelers, artists, and musicians from all over the world, who were looking for a free and alternative lifestyle. Some of the famous visitors of Matala Beach include Bob Dylan, Joni Mitchell, Cat Stevens, and Janis Joplin. The hippie spirit is still alive in Matala Beach, which hosts an annual music festival, featuring rock, folk, and reggae bands, as well as various events, such as workshops, yoga, and meditation.

Matala Beach is not only a place of history and culture, but also a place of beauty and nature. It is located in a scenic bay, surrounded by hills and rocks, and it has a long and sandy beach, with clear and turquoise water. The beach is ideal for swimming, sunbathing, or relaxing, and it offers many facilities and services, such as sun loungers, umbrellas, showers, toilets, and lifeguards. The beach is also a protected area, as it is part of the Natura 2000 network, and it hosts many rare and endangered species of plants and animals, such as the loggerhead sea turtle, the Cretan palm, and the Cretan wild goat.

Diktaion (Psychro) Cave

Diktaion (Psychro) Cave is a magnificent and sacred cave, located on the slopes of Mount Dikti, in the Lasithi Plateau, in the eastern part of Crete. It is one of the most important and visited archaeological sites on the island, as it is associated with the myth of the birth of Zeus, the king of the Greek gods.

According to the legend, Zeus was the son of Cronus and Rhea, the rulers of the Titans, the primordial gods who preceded the Olympians. Cronus had a prophecy that one of his children would overthrow him, so he swallowed them all as soon as they were born. Rhea, who was pregnant with Zeus, managed to deceive Cronus and gave him a stone wrapped in a cloth instead of the baby. She then hid Zeus in a cave, where he was nursed by a goat named Amalthea and protected by the Curetes, a group of warriors who clashed their shields to cover the cries of the infant.

Diktaion Cave is believed to be the cave where Zeus was born and raised, and where he later returned to mate with Europa, the mother of Minos, the legendary king of Crete. The cave was also a place of worship and pilgrimage for the ancient Cretans, who considered it the most sacred spot on the island. The cave was used as a shrine from the Early Minoan to the Roman period, and many votive offerings, such as pottery, bronze, iron, and bone objects, were found inside. The cave also contains a stalagmite altar, where sacrifices and rituals were performed.

The cave is open to the public, and it can be reached by car or by foot from the nearby village of Psychro. The cave has two chambers, the upper and the lower, which are connected by a staircase. The upper chamber is the larger and more impressive, with a height of 10 meters and a diameter of 40 meters. The lower chamber is smaller and darker, with a depth of 25 meters and a diameter of 14 meters. The cave is full of stalactites and stalagmites, which create a spectacular and mysterious atmosphere. The cave also has an underground lake, which is the source of the river Aposelemis.

80

Chapter 6 • Accommodation Recommendations

Villa Recommendations

A villa is a perfect choice for families, couples, or groups of friends, who want to have their own space, amenities, and facilities, such as a private pool, a garden, a kitchen, and a living room. A villa also allows you to experience the authentic and traditional Cretan lifestyle, as you can stay in a village, interact with the locals, and enjoy the local cuisine. A villa also gives you the freedom to explore the island at your own pace, as you can rent a car and visit different places, without being tied to a hotel schedule or location. Below are some recommendations:

Best Villa in Crete: Winehill Villa. This is a stunning villa, located in the hills near Chania, with panoramic views of the sea and the mountains. The villa has four bedrooms, four bathrooms, a spacious living room, a fully-equipped kitchen, and a dining area. The villa also has a large outdoor area, with a private pool, a jacuzzi, a barbecue, a playground, and a terrace. The villa is elegantly decorated, with modern and luxurious furnishings, and it offers many amenities, such as air conditioning, heating, Wi-Fi, satellite TV, DVD player, and fireplace. The villa is ideal for families or groups of friends, who want to have a relaxing and comfortable stay, in a peaceful and scenic setting.

Best Villa for Beach Lovers: Velvet Breeze. This is a cozy and charming villa, located in the village of Plaka, near the beach of Almyrida. The villa has two bedrooms, two bathrooms, a living room, a kitchen, and a dining area. The villa also has a lovely outdoor area, with a private pool, a sun deck, a garden, and a balcony. The villa is tastefully decorated, with bright and cheerful colors, and it offers many amenities, such as air conditioning, heating, Wi-Fi, satellite TV, DVD player, and washing machine. The villa is ideal for couples or small families, who want to have a beach holiday, in a quiet and friendly village.

Best Villa for Families: Green Diamond. This is a spacious and modern villa, located in the village of Agia Triada, near the town of Rethymno. The villa has three bedrooms, three bathrooms, a living room, a kitchen, and a dining area. The villa also has a fantastic outdoor area, with a private pool, a jacuzzi, a barbecue, a playground, and a terrace. The villa is stylishly decorated, with contemporary and minimalist furnishings, and it offers many amenities, such as air conditioning, heating, Wi-Fi, satellite TV, DVD player, and fireplace. The villa is ideal for families with children, who want to have a fun and comfortable stay, in a convenient and safe location.

Best Villa for Luxury Lovers: Cavo Dago. This is a spectacular villa, located on a cliff near the town of Agios Nikolaos, with breathtaking views of the sea and the island of Spinalonga. The villa has five bedrooms, five bathrooms, a living room, a kitchen, and a dining area. The villa also has an amazing outdoor area, with a private pool, a jacuzzi, a sauna, a gym, a bar, and a terrace. The villa is exquisitely decorated, with sophisticated and elegant furnishings, and it offers many amenities, such as air conditioning, heating, Wi-Fi, satellite TV, DVD player, and fireplace. The villa is ideal for couples or groups of friends, who want to have a luxurious and exclusive stay, in a stunning and romantic setting.

Best Villa with Swimming Pool: Elounda Luxury. This is a magnificent villa, located in the resort of

Elounda, near the beach and the town of Agios Nikolaos. The villa has four bedrooms, four bathrooms, a living room, a kitchen, and a dining area. The villa also has a wonderful outdoor area, with a private pool, a jacuzzi, a barbecue, a garden, and a terrace. The villa is beautifully decorated, with classic and refined furnishings, and it offers many amenities, such as air conditioning, heating, Wi-Fi, satellite TV, DVD player, and fireplace. The villa is ideal for families or groups of friends, who want to have a relaxing and enjoyable stay, in a prestigious and convenient location.

Best Villa in Heraklion: Nefeli. This is a lovely villa, located in the village of Agia Pelagia, near the beach and the city of Heraklion. The villa has three bedrooms, two bathrooms, a living room, a kitchen, and a dining area. The villa also has a nice outdoor area, with a private pool, a sun deck, a garden, and a balcony. The villa is simply decorated, with cozy and rustic furnishings, and it offers many amenities, such as air conditioning, heating, Wi-Fi, satellite TV, DVD player, and washing machine. The villa is ideal for couples or small families, who want to have a beach holiday, in a calm and relaxing village.

Best Villa in Rethymno: White Grace. This is a

stunning villa, located in the village of Asteri, near the beach and the town of Rethymno. The villa has four bedrooms, four bathrooms, a living room, a kitchen, and a dining area. The villa also has a superb outdoor area, with a private pool, a jacuzzi, a barbecue, a playground, and a terrace. The villa is elegantly decorated, with white and gray tones, and it offers many amenities, such as air conditioning, heating, Wi-Fi, satellite TV, DVD player, and fireplace. The villa is ideal for families or groups of friends, who want to have a stylish and comfortable stay, in a serene and scenic location.

Hotel Recommendations

A hotel is a great choice for solo travelers, couples, or groups of friends, who want to have a hassle-free and enjoyable stay, with access to facilities and amenities, such as a pool, a spa, a restaurant, and a bar. A hotel also allows you to experience the hospitality and the culture of Crete, as you can interact with the staff, the locals, and other guests. A hotel also gives you the opportunity to explore the island, as you can book tours, excursions, or activities, through the hotel or nearby agencies. Below are some recommendations:

Best Hotel in Crete: Casa Delfino Hotel & Spa.

This is a five-star hotel, located in the heart of Chania, the second largest and most picturesque city on the island, with a beautiful old town, a Venetian harbor, and a lively nightlife. The hotel is housed in a 17th-century Venetian mansion, which was once the home of a noble family, and it has been restored and renovated with elegance and luxury. The hotel has 24 rooms and suites, each with a unique design and character, and some with private terraces or jacuzzis. The hotel also has a rooftop terrace, with stunning views of the city and the sea, a spa, a restaurant, and a bar. The hotel offers many services and amenities, such as air conditioning, heating, Wi-Fi, satellite TV, DVD player, and fireplace. The hotel is ideal for couples or groups of friends, who want to have a relaxing and comfortable stay, in a historic and scenic setting.

Best Hotel for Beach Lovers: Out of the Blue Resort & Spa. This is a four-star resort, located in the village of Plaka, near the beach of Almyrida, on the north coast of Crete. The resort has 51 rooms and suites, each with a balcony or a terrace, and some with a private pool or a jacuzzi. The resort also has a large outdoor pool, a spa, a gym, a restaurant, and a bar. The resort offers many services and amenities, such as air conditioning, heating, Wi-Fi, satellite TV, DVD player, and washing machine. The resort is ideal for couples or small families, who want to have a beach holiday, in a quiet and friendly village.

Best Apartment in Crete: Dimitris Apartments. This is a stunning apartment, located in the seaside village of Bali, on the north coast of Crete, within 75 metres from the beach. The apartment has two bedrooms, one bathroom, a spacious living room, a fully-equipped kitchen, and a balcony with sea or garden views. The apartment also has free Wi-Fi, satellite TV, air conditioning, and a washing machine. The apartment is ideal for families or groups of friends, who want to have a relaxing and comfortable stay, in a peaceful and scenic setting.

Guesthouse Recommendations

A guesthouse is a great choice for solo travelers, couples, or groups of friends, who want to have a more personal and intimate stay, with access to local tips and insights, as well as homemade breakfasts and snacks. A guesthouse also allows you to experience the traditional and rural Cretan lifestyle, as you can stay in a village, interact with the locals, and enjoy the local cuisine. A guesthouse also gives you the opportunity to explore the island, as you can rent a car and visit different places, without being tied to a hotel location or schedule. Below are some recommendations:

Best Guesthouse in Crete: Arodamos Traditional Houses. This is a stunning guesthouse, located in the hills near Chania, with panoramic views of the sea and the mountains. The guesthouse consists of six traditional stone houses, each with a fireplace, a kitchenette, and a balcony or patio. The guesthouse also has a common area, with a pool, a jacuzzi, a playground, and a terrace. The guesthouse offers many services and amenities, such as air conditioning, heating, Wi-Fi, satellite TV, and DVD player. The guesthouse is ideal for families or groups of friends, who want to have a relaxing and comfortable stay, in a peaceful and scenic setting.

Best Guesthouse in Chania: Ionas Boutique Hotel. This is a lovely guesthouse, located in the heart of Chania, the second largest and most picturesque city on the island, with a beautiful old town, a Venetian harbor, and a lively nightlife. The guesthouse is housed in a 16th-century Ottoman-style townhouse, where rooms are cool in white and exposed stone. The guesthouse also has a pergola-shaded terrace, where

88

breakfast is served. The guesthouse offers many services and amenities, such as air conditioning, heating, Wi-Fi, satellite TV, and DVD player. The guesthouse is ideal for couples or groups of friends, who want to have a cultural and historical stay, in a charming and central location.

Best Guesthouse in Heraklion: Crete Garden Guesthouse. This is a cozy and modern guesthouse, located in the village of Alevriko, near the beach and the city of Heraklion, the largest and most vibrant city on the island, with a rich archaeological and cultural heritage. The guesthouse consists of two bedrooms, a bathroom, a living room, a kitchen, and a dining area. The guesthouse also has a nice outdoor area, with a garden and a balcony. The guesthouse is simply decorated, with cozy and rustic furnishings, and it offers many amenities, such as air conditioning, heating, Wi-Fi, satellite TV, DVD player, and washing machine. The guesthouse is ideal for couples or small families, who want to have a beach holiday, in a calm and relaxing village.

Best Guesthouse in Rethymno: Casa Vitae. This is a gorgeous guesthouse, located in the old town of Rethymno, the third largest and most historic city on the island, with a medieval fortress, a Venetian port, and a lively atmosphere. The guesthouse is housed in a 15th-century Ottoman-Venetian era townhouse, where rooms are atmospheric with stone walls, wooden floors, and raftered ceilings. The guesthouse also has a courtyard, where breakfast is served. The guesthouse offers many services and amenities, such as air conditioning, heating, Wi-Fi, satellite TV, and DVD player. The guesthouse is ideal for couples or groups of friends, who want to have a romantic and elegant stay, in a historic and scenic location.

Chapter 7 • Cretan Cuisine and Food Experiences

Introduction to Cretan Cuisine

Cretan cuisine is the culinary expression of the rich culture and history of the Mediterranean island of Crete. It is a cuisine that reflects the diversity of the land, the sea, and the seasons, as well as the influences of various civilizations that have left their mark on the island over the centuries.

Cretan cuisine is based on the principles of the Mediterranean diet, which is considered one of the healthiest in the world. It is a cuisine that celebrates the natural flavors and aromas of fresh, local, and seasonal ingredients, such as olive oil, herbs, vegetables, fruits, grains, legumes, cheese, yogurt, honey, nuts, fish, seafood, and meat. It is a cuisine that uses simple but creative methods of preparation, such as grilling, baking, boiling, frying, and stewing, to create dishes that are satisfying, nutritious, and delicious.

Cretan cuisine is also a cuisine that reflects the spirit and character of the Cretan people, who are known for their hospitality, generosity, and love of life. It is a cuisine that invites you to share and enjoy the food with family and friends, accompanied by wine, raki, or ouzo, and often followed by music, dancing, and storytelling. It is a cuisine that offers you a taste of the authentic and unique Cretan way of living.

In this guide, you will discover the traditional Cretan food specialties that you must try during your visit to Crete, such as dakos, snails, kalitsounia, gamopilafo, staka, apaki, boureki, horta, dolmades, and many more.

Famous Cretan Dishes

Cretan cuisine uses fresh, local, and seasonal ingredients, such as olive oil, herbs, vegetables, fruits, grains, legumes, cheese, yogurt, honey, nuts, fish, seafood, and meat. Cretan cuisine also incorporates influences from different cultures that have interacted with the island over the centuries, such as the Minoans, the Byzantines, the Venetians, and the Turks.

Dakos

Dakos is a simple but satisfying appetizer or snack, consisting of a dry barley rusk called paximadi, topped with crumbled myzithra cheese, chopped ripe tomatoes, whole olives, capers, fresh oregano, and a generous drizzle of high-quality olive oil. It is sometimes rubbed with a clove of garlic and sprinkled with sea salt for extra flavor. Dakos is also known as ntakos or koukouvagia, and it is a typical dish of the Cretan diet, as it uses ingredients that are readily available and easy to preserve. Dakos is best enjoyed with a glass of wine, raki, or ouzo, and it is a perfect example of how Cretan cuisine transforms simple ingredients into a delicious and nutritious dish.

Graviera Kritis

Graviera Kritis is the best-known and most popular cheese of Crete, and it has a long history and tradition. It is a hard, yellow cheese with a firm texture and a nutty flavor, and it is made from sheep milk or a mixture of sheep and goat milk. The milk comes from animals that graze freely on the green pastures of the island, and their diet is based on local plants, which give their milk a special quality. Graviera Kritis is produced using traditional methods and ripened in facilities in four prefectures of Crete: Hania, Rethymnos, Iraklion, and Lasithio. Graviera Kritis is a versatile cheese that can be eaten as a table cheese, grated over pasta or salads, or fried as saganaki. It is also an excellent accompaniment to honey, nuts, and fruits.

Staka me ayga

Staka me ayga is a simple but hearty breakfast dish, consisting of eggs cooked with staka, a type of buttery cream mixed with flour. Staka is a unique specialty of Cretan cuisine, and it is made from the fat that rises to the surface of boiled sheep or goat milk. Staka is cooked with flour and salt until it thickens and separates from the butter, which is then used to fry or poach the eggs. The dish is seasoned with salt and pepper, and it is often paired with apaki, a smoked pork meat. Staka me ayga is a rich and filling dish that provides energy and warmth for the day ahead.

Sfakianopita

Sfakianopita is a traditional Cretan treat that resembles a thin pancake or crepe, filled with soft white cheese. The dough is made with flour, olive oil, water, salt, and a shot of raki, a local distilled spirit. The cheese is usually myzithra, a fresh whey cheese that is kneaded with the dough. The whole combination is then flattened out into a thin circle and fried until golden and crispy. Sfakianopita is also known as sfakiani pita or mizithropita, and it is believed to have been created by the shepherds of Sfakia, a mountainous region in the south of Crete. Sfakianopita is a sweet and savory delicacy that can be eaten as a snack or dessert, drizzled with honey or sprinkled with sugar and cinnamon.

Myzithra

Myzithra is another traditional cheese of Crete, made from the whey of sheep or goat milk cheeses. It is a soft, white, and crumbly cheese with a mild and slightly sour taste. It is similar to ricotta, but with a lower moisture content and a firmer texture. Myzithra is a versatile cheese that can be used in various dishes, such as pies, salads, pasta, or desserts. It can also be eaten as a table cheese, spread on bread, or sprinkled with honey and nuts. Myzithra is a low-fat and high-protein cheese that is rich in calcium and vitamins.

Kalitsounia

Kalitsounia are small pies or pastries that are typical of Cretan cuisine. They are made with thin sheets of dough that are filled with various ingredients and then folded into different shapes. The most common fillings are cheese, greens, herbs, or sweet cheese and honey. Kalitsounia can be baked, fried, or boiled, depending on the filling and the region. Kalitsounia are usually eaten as appetizers, snacks, or desserts, and they are often served with honey, yogurt, or sugar. Kalitsounia are also known as lychnarakia, pichtogalo, or sarikopites, and they are a festive dish that is prepared for Easter, weddings, or other celebrations.

Gamopilafo

Gamopilafo is a traditional Cretan dish that is served at weddings and other special occasions. It is a rice pilaf cooked with meat broth, butter, and lemon juice, and it is usually accompanied by boiled or roasted meat, such as lamb, goat, or chicken. Gamopilafo is a rich and flavorful dish that symbolizes abundance and prosperity, and it is considered a delicacy by the Cretans. Gamopilafo is also known as pilafi, and it is similar to the Turkish pilav or the Italian risotto, but with a distinct Cretan touch.

Apaki

Apaki is a smoked pork meat that is a specialty of Cretan cuisine. It is made from lean pork meat that is cut into small pieces and marinated in vinegar, salt, herbs, and spices. The meat is then smoked with aromatic wood, such as sage, thyme, or oregano, and dried in the sun or in a special oven. Apaki is a tender and tasty meat that can be eaten as a snack, appetizer, or main course. It can also be added to salads, pies, or eggs, or cooked with vegetables, wine, or honey. Apaki is a preserved meat that can last for a long time, and it is a good source of protein and iron.

Boureki

Boureki is a savory pie or casserole that is made with layers of zucchini, potatoes, cheese, and mint, and baked in the oven with olive oil and cream. Boureki is a typical dish of the city of Hania, and it is usually eaten as a main course or a side dish. Boureki is a filling and satisfying dish that showcases the freshness and simplicity of Cretan cuisine. Boureki is also known as boureki Haniotiko, and it is similar to the Greek moussaka, but without meat or bechamel sauce.

Horta

Horta is a generic term for wild or cultivated greens that are widely used in Cretan cuisine. Horta can include various types of greens, such as spinach, chard, dandelion, chicory, nettles, purslane, amaranth, and many more. Horta are usually boiled or steamed, and then seasoned with olive oil, lemon juice, salt, and pepper. They can also be cooked with other ingredients, such as potatoes, beans, eggs, cheese, or meat. Horta are a staple of the Cretan diet, as they are abundant, cheap, and nutritious. They are rich in fiber, antioxidants, vitamins, and minerals, and they have a bitter and refreshing taste that balances the richness of other dishes.

Famous Cretan Drinks

Below are some of the most famous and representative drinks of Cretan cuisine, which you should not miss during your visit to the island.

Tsikoudia

Tsikoudia, also known as raki, is the national drink of Crete and one of the most popular alcoholic beverages in Greece. It is a clear, strong spirit that is distilled from the fermented grape pomace, the solid remains that are left after the grapes have been pressed for wine making. Tsikoudia is traditionally distilled in October and November, usually in small copper stills, and it has an alcohol content of around 40%. Tsikoudia is often flavored with herbs, such as sage, thyme, or oregano, or fruits, such as lemon, orange, or fig. Tsikoudia is usually served in small glasses, either chilled or at room temperature, and it is often accompanied by meze, small dishes of cheese, olives, nuts, or dried fruits. Tsikoudia is a drink that symbolizes the hospitality, friendship, and joy of the Cretan people, and it is often offered as a welcoming gesture or a farewell gift to guests.

Rakomelo

Rakomelo is a Cretan drink that combines honey and

tsikoudia, a clear Cretan spirit that is sometimes referred to as raki, though it is not anise-flavored like the namesake Turkish spirit. The drink is often flavored with herbs and spices, such as cinnamon, cardamom, or cloves. Rakomelo is usually served hot, especially in winter, and it is believed to have medicinal properties, such as soothing sore throats, warming the body, and aiding digestion. Rakomelo is also a popular drink for celebrations, such as weddings, christenings, or festivals, and it is often enjoyed with music, dancing, and singing.

Vidiano

Vidiano is a native white grape from Crete that produces elegant and aromatic white wines. It is mostly cultivated around Rethymnon, and it is considered one of the most promising and quality grape varieties in Greece. Vidiano wines are usually dry, with a pale yellow color and a floral and fruity bouquet, with notes of peach, apricot, citrus, and honey. Vidiano wines are well-balanced, with a medium body and a refreshing acidity, and they pair well with seafood, cheese, or salads. Vidiano wines are a great example of the revival and innovation of the Cretan wine industry, which has a long and rich history dating back to the Minoan civilization.

Kostifali

Kostifali is another indigenous red grape from Crete that produces robust and spicy red wines. It is mainly grown in the Heraklion region, and it is often blended with other grape varieties, such as Syrah, Merlot, or Mandilari, to enhance its color, acidity, and complexity. Kostifali wines are usually dry, with a ruby red color and a peppery and fruity aroma, with hints of cherry, plum, and leather. Kostifali wines are full-bodied, with a high alcohol content and a smooth tannin structure, and they match well with meat, cheese, or pasta dishes. Kostifali wines are a reflection of the terroir and the tradition of Crete, which has a diverse and fertile soil and a favorable climate for viticulture.

Soumada

Soumada is a non-alcoholic, syrupy, almond-based beverage that is produced on the island of Crete. It is made with a mixture of fresh, locally-grown almonds, sugar, and water, which is simmered in sugar syrup to create this signature Cretan drink. Soumada is usually served cold, in tall glasses, and it is often garnished with almonds, cinnamon, or rose petals. Soumada is a sweet and refreshing drink that can be enjoyed as a snack or a dessert, and it is also a popular drink for weddings and other celebrations, as it symbolizes happiness and prosperity.

Vilana

Vilana is a white grape variety native to Crete that produces crisp and light white wines. It is a very productive and resistant grape that is widely grown in the Lasithi and Heraklion regions. Vilana wines are usually dry, with a straw yellow color and a delicate and floral aroma, with notes of apple, pear, and citrus. Vilana wines are low in alcohol and acidity, and they are best consumed young and chilled. Vilana wines are a perfect accompaniment to fish, seafood, or vegetable dishes, and they are a representation of the freshness and simplicity of Cretan cuisine.

Mournoraki

Mournoraki is a rare Cretan spirit that is distilled from black mulberries. It is usually quite potent, and it is mostly enjoyed as a welcoming drink, but it also works well as an aperitif or a digestif. Mournoraki is not easily found on the market, as it is mostly produced by local farmers or families for their own consumption or for special occasions. Mournoraki has a dark color and a fruity and sweet flavor, with a slight bitterness and a smooth finish. Mournoraki is a unique and authentic

Cretan drink that showcases the diversity and creativity of the island's distillation tradition.

Wine and Food Pairing

Cretan wines are a perfect match for the local cuisine, which is based on the Mediterranean diet and uses fresh, seasonal, and organic ingredients. Below are some tips and suggestions on how to pair Cretan wines with Cretan dishes, so that you can enjoy the best of both worlds.

White Wines

Cretan white wines are usually dry, crisp, and aromatic, with flavors of citrus, apple, pear, peach, apricot, and honey. They are ideal for hot summer days, as they are refreshing and light. They also pair well with seafood, fish, cheese, salads, and vegetable dishes, as they enhance their freshness and flavor. Some of the most popular white grape varieties in Crete are:

Vidiano: Vidiano wines pair well with fried zucchini flowers, Cretan boureki (a pie with zucchini, potatoes, cheese, and mint), and wild greens.

Vilana: Vilana wines pair well with fish, seafood, or vegetable dishes, such as grilled octopus, stuffed vine leaves, or Cretan dakos (a barley rusk topped with tomato, cheese, olives, and herbs).

Muscat of Spina: Muscat of Spina wines pair well with desserts, such as yogurt with honey and nuts, cheese pies, or baklava.

Red Wines

Cretan red wines are usually dry, robust, and spicy, with flavors of cherry, plum, blackberry, pepper, and leather. They are ideal for cold winter nights, as they are warming and full-bodied. They also pair well with meat, cheese, pasta, and mushroom dishes, as they complement their richness and texture. Some of the most common red grape varieties in Crete are:

Kotsifali: Kotsifali wines pair well with loukaniko (a Greek country-style sausage), grilled lamb chops, and chicken souvlaki.

Mandilari: Mandilari wines pair well with game, cheese, or pasta dishes, such as rabbit stew, graviera cheese, or spaghetti with meat sauce.

Liatiko: Liatiko wines pair well with chocolate, nuts, or dried fruits, such as chocolate cake, walnuts, or figs.

Rosé Wines

Cretan rosé wines are usually dry, refreshing, and fruity, with flavors of strawberry, raspberry, watermelon, and rose. They are ideal for spring and autumn days, as they are versatile and easy to drink. They also pair well with a variety of dishes, such as cheese, salads, pizza, or meatballs, as they balance their acidity and sweetness. Some of the most popular rosé grape varieties in Crete are:

Syrah: Syrah rosé wines pair well with cheese, salads, or pizza, such as feta cheese, Greek salad, or margherita pizza.

Grenache: Grenache rosé wines pair well with meat, cheese, or pasta dishes, such as keftedes (Greek meatballs), anthotyro cheese, or penne with tomato sauce.

Romeiko: Romeiko rosé wines pair well with mushroom, cheese, or meat dishes, such as mushroom risotto, staka (a buttery cream mixed with flour), or apaki (a smoked pork meat).

Sparkling Wines

Cretan sparkling wines are usually dry, bubbly, and festive, with flavors of apple, pear, lemon, and bread. They are ideal for celebrations, as they are fun and lively. They also pair well with appetizers, seafood, cheese, or desserts, as they cleanse the palate and add sparkle to the food. Some of the most common sparkling wine varieties in Crete are:

Chardonnay: Chardonnay sparkling wines pair well with appetizers, seafood, or cheese, such as smoked salmon, oysters, or brie cheese.

Moschofilero: Moschofilero sparkling wines pair well with seafood, cheese, or desserts, such as shrimp, feta cheese, or fruit salad.

Plito: Plito sparkling wines pair well with appetizers, seafood, or cheese, such as olives, mussels, or myzithra cheese.

As you can see, Crete has a lot to offer to wine lovers, as it has a diverse and quality wine production that can satisfy every preference and occasion. By following our wine and food pairing suggestions, you can enhance your gastronomic experience and discover the authentic and unique flavors of Cretan cuisine. Cheers!

Must-Visit Cretan Restaurants and Cafes

Below are some recommendations for must-visit Cretan restaurants and cafes:

Portela Pool Bar, Kastri

If you are looking for a relaxing and scenic spot to enjoy a refreshing drink, a light snack, or a delicious meal, Portela Pool Bar is the place for you. Located in the village of Keratokambos, Portela Pool Bar is part of the Portela Apartments complex, which offers comfortable and affordable accommodation with stunning views of the sea and the mountains. Portela Pool Bar has a large and inviting pool, surrounded by sunbeds and umbrellas, where you can cool off and soak up the sun. The bar also has a spacious and shaded terrace, where you can sit and enjoy the breeze and the panorama. Portela Pool Bar serves a variety of drinks, such as coffee, juice, beer, wine, and cocktails, as well as snacks, such as sandwiches, salads, burgers, and pizzas. The bar also offers a daily menu of homemade Cretan dishes, such as dakos, snails, kalitsounia, gamopilafo, staka, apaki, boureki, horta, and dolmades. Portela Pool Bar is open from April to October, from 8:30 am to 11:00 pm.

Krotiri Restaurant, Agios Nikolaos

If you are looking for a fine dining experience with a spectacular view, Krotiri Restaurant is the place for you. Located on the beach of Salonikiou, Krotiri Restaurant is part of the Krotiri Resort, a luxury hotel that offers elegant and spacious rooms and suites with private pools and jacuzzis. Krotiri Restaurant has a stylish and romantic setting, with a spacious and airy dining room and a charming and cozy terrace, overlooking the sea and the island of Spinalonga. Krotiri Restaurant serves a variety of dishes, inspired by the Greek and Mediterranean cuisine, with a creative and contemporary twist. The restaurant uses fresh, local, and seasonal ingredients, such as olive oil, herbs, vegetables, fruits, grains, cheese, honey, nuts, fish, seafood, and meat, to create dishes that are satisfying, nutritious, and delicious. Some of the dishes that you can try at Krotiri Restaurant are: grilled octopus with fava and capers, lamb chops with rosemary and thyme, sea bass with lemon and olive oil, and chocolate souffle with vanilla ice cream. Krotiri Restaurant also has an extensive wine list, featuring wines from Greece and other countries, as well as a selection of cocktails and spirits. Krotiri Restaurant is open from May to October, from 1:00 pm to 11:00 pm.

Talos Restaurant, Kato Daratso

If you are looking for a family-friendly and budget-friendly place to enjoy a hearty and tasty meal, Talos Restaurant is the place for you. Located on the main street of Kato Daratso, Talos Restaurant is a casual and friendly place, with a large and colorful dining room and a lively and cheerful atmosphere. Talos Restaurant serves a variety of dishes, based on the traditional

Cretan cuisine, with a touch of modernity and innovation. The restaurant uses simple but quality ingredients, such as olive oil, herbs, vegetables, fruits, grains, legumes, cheese, yogurt, honey, nuts, fish, seafood, and meat, to create dishes that are satisfying, nutritious, and delicious. Some of the dishes that you can try at Talos Restaurant are: peinerli with kimas (a boat-shaped pizza with minced lamb), grilled sea bream with lemon and olive oil, chicken souvlaki with pita and tzatziki, and yogurt with honey and nuts. Talos Restaurant also has a daily menu of homemade Cretan dishes, such as dakos, snails, kalitsounia, gamopilafo, staka, apaki, boureki, horta, and dolmades. Talos Restaurant is open from April to October, from 8:30 am to 11:00 pm.

To Mikro Livadi Residences & Family Restaurant, Episkopi

If you are looking for a cozy and charming place to enjoy a relaxing and delicious meal, To Mikro Livadi Residences & Family Restaurant is the place for you. Located on the beach of Episkopi, To Mikro Livadi Residences & Family Restaurant is part of the To Mikro Livadi Special Lodges, which offers a garden and a sun terrace, as well as an eco salt water pool. To Mikro

Livadi Residences & Family Restaurant has a rustic and elegant setting, with a wooden and stone dining room and a lovely and shaded terrace, facing the sea and the pool. To Mikro Livadi Residences & Family Restaurant serves a variety of dishes, based on the Cretan cuisine, with a focus on organic and local products. The restaurant uses fresh, local, and organic ingredients, such as olive oil, herbs, vegetables, fruits, grains, legumes, cheese, yogurt, honey, nuts, fish, seafood, and meat, to create dishes that are satisfying, nutritious, and delicious. Some of the dishes that you can try at To Mikro Livadi Residences & Family Restaurant are: grilled octopus with fava and capers, lamb chops with rosemary and thyme, sea bass with lemon and olive oil, and chocolate souffle with vanilla ice cream. To Mikro Livadi Residences & Family Restaurant also has a daily menu of homemade Cretan dishes, such as dakos, snails, kalitsounia, gamopilafo, staka, apaki, boureki, horta, and dolmades. To Mikro Livadi Residences & Family Restaurant is open from April to October, from 1:00 pm to 11:30 pm.

Culinary Experiences and Cooking Classes

Below are some of the best culinary experiences and cooking classes that you can enjoy in Crete:

The Real Cretan Cooking Experience

This is one of the most popular cooking classes in Crete, where you can learn how to cook like a local with pure Cretan ingredients and live a unique culinary experience. The class takes place in a serene house in the hills, surrounded by nature and with stunning views of the sea and the mountains. You will be welcomed by a friendly and knowledgeable guide, who will introduce you to the Cretan cuisine and culture. You will then prepare your own meal, using fresh and organic ingredients that you will pick from the garden or the farm. You will learn how to make five different recipes of traditional Cretan dishes, such as dakos, snails, kalitsounia, gamopilafo, staka, apaki, boureki, horta, and dolmades. You will also have the chance to feed the goats and sheep, taste local wines and spirits, and learn about the history and tradition of Crete. After cooking, you will enjoy your meal with your guide and the other participants, sharing stories and laughter. The class lasts for about six hours, and it includes transportation, ingredients, equipment, recipes, drinks, and lunch. The price is 122€ per adult and 61€ per child.

Cretan Cooking Classes

This is another excellent cooking class in Crete, where you can experience the Cretan gastronomy, learn to create healthy dishes, and have fun and interactive cooking sessions. The class takes place in a traditional Cretan village, called Tersana, where you will be greeted by a friendly and experienced chef, who will guide you through the cooking process. You will learn how to make five different recipes of traditional Cretan dishes, such as dakos, snails, kalitsounia, gamopilafo, staka, apaki, boureki, horta, and dolmades. You will also learn about the nutritional value and the health benefits of the Cretan diet, as well as the history and culture behind each dish. After cooking, you will enjoy your meal with your chef and the other participants, accompanied by local wine and raki. The class lasts for about four hours, and it includes transportation, ingredients, equipment, recipes, drinks, and lunch. The price is 122€ per adult and 61€ per child.

Santorini Gastronomy - Cooking classes & more

This is a unique and exclusive cooking class in Crete,

where you can learn how to cook Cretan dishes with a twist of Santorini flavors and ingredients. The class takes place in a beautiful and modern villa, located in Firostefani, where you will be welcomed by a professional and passionate chef, who will introduce you to the Mediterranean cuisine and the Santorini gastronomy. You will learn how to make four different recipes of Cretan dishes, such as dakos, snails, kalitsounia, and gamopilafo, using fresh and organic ingredients from Santorini, such as cherry tomatoes, fava beans, capers, and white eggplant. You will also learn about the volcanic soil and the microclimate of Santorini, and how they affect the quality and the taste of the products. After cooking, you will enjoy your meal with your chef and the other participants, paired with local wines and spirits. The class lasts for about three hours, and it includes transportation, ingredients, equipment, recipes, drinks, and lunch. The price is 150€ per adult and 75€ per child.

Chapter 8 • Outdoor Activities and Nature

Hiking and Trekking in Crete

Crete is a paradise for hiking and trekking enthusiasts, as it offers a wide range of trails and routes that will challenge your skills and reward your senses. The island has a diverse and stunning landscape, ranging from high mountains and deep gorges to vast plateaus and golden beaches. Crete also has a rich and ancient history and culture, which you can discover along the way. Whether you are looking for a short and easy walk or a long and strenuous adventure, you will find something to suit your preferences and abilities in Crete. Below are some of the best hiking and trekking experiences that you can enjoy in Crete:

Samaria Gorge

Samaria Gorge is one of the most famous and popular hiking destinations in Crete and Europe. It is the longest gorge in Europe, with a length of 16 km, and it is part of the Samaria National Park, a UNESCO Biosphere Reserve. The hike starts from the village of Omalos, at an altitude of 1,250 m, and ends at the coastal village of

Agia Roumeli, at sea level. The hike takes about 6 to 8 hours, depending on your pace and fitness level, and it is considered moderately difficult. Along the way, you will enjoy the spectacular scenery of the gorge, with its towering cliffs, narrow passages, and diverse flora and fauna. You will also pass by the abandoned village of Samaria, the Byzantine chapel of Agios Nikolaos, and the famous Iron Gates, the narrowest point of the gorge, where the walls are only 3 m apart. Samaria Gorge is open from May to October, and you need to pay an entrance fee of 5€. You also need to wear comfortable shoes, carry enough water and food, and follow the rules and signs of the park.

Imbros Gorge

Imbros Gorge is another beautiful and popular gorge in Crete, located in the region of Sfakia. It is shorter and easier than Samaria Gorge, with a length of 8 km and a duration of 2 to 3 hours. The hike starts from the village of Imbros, at an altitude of 780 m, and ends at the village of Komitades, at an altitude of 200 m. The hike is suitable for all ages and skill levels, and it is ideal for families and beginners. Along the way, you will admire the impressive scenery of the gorge, with its rocky walls, shady trees, and colorful flowers. You will also pass by several narrow sections, where the walls are only 2 m apart, and encounter some springs, caves, and ruins. Imbros Gorge is open all year round, and you need to pay an entrance fee of 2.5€. You also need to wear comfortable shoes, carry enough water and food, and respect the nature and the locals.

Preveli Beach

Preveli Beach is one of the most beautiful and exotic beaches in Crete, located in the south coast of the island. It is also known as Palm Beach, because of the large palm forest that grows along the river that flows into the sea. The beach is accessible by boat from the nearby villages of Plakias and Agia Galini, or by car from the village of Lefkogia. However, the best way to reach the beach is by hiking from the Monastery of Preveli, a historic and religious site that overlooks the beach. The hike is about 4 km long and takes about 1.5 hours. It is relatively easy, but it involves some steep and rocky sections, as well as some river crossings. Along the way, you will enjoy the stunning views of the sea and the mountains, as well as the lush and tropical vegetation of the palm forest. Once you reach the beach, you can relax on the sand, swim in the crystal clear water, or explore the river and the palm forest. Preveli Beach is open all year round, but it is advisable to avoid the peak summer months, as it can get very crowded and hot.

Lassithi Plateau

Lassithi Plateau is a large and fertile plain, located in the east of Crete, at an altitude of 850 m. It is surrounded by the Dikti Mountains, and it is famous for its traditional windmills, which used to irrigate the crops. The plateau is also known for its archaeological and mythological significance, as it is the birthplace of Zeus, the king of the Greek gods, according to the legend. The plateau is accessible by car from the towns of Agios Nikolaos and Heraklion, or by bus from the village of Malia. However, the best way to explore the plateau is by hiking or cycling, as there are many trails and routes that connect the villages and the sights of the area. Some of the highlights of the plateau are the Dikteon Cave, where Zeus was born and hidden from his father Cronus, the Monastery of Kera, which has a beautiful collection of frescoes and icons, and the Eco Park, which has a museum, a farm, and a restaurant. The plateau is open all year round, and it offers a variety of activities and experiences, such as horse riding, pottery, cheese making, and wine tasting.

E4 European Path

E4 European Path is a long-distance hiking trail that crosses Europe from west to east, starting from Spain and ending in Cyprus. The trail passes through Crete, covering about 500 km of the island, from Kissamos in the west to Zakros in the east. The trail follows the coastline, the mountains, and the gorges of Crete, offering a diverse and challenging terrain, as well as stunning views and cultural attractions. The trail is divided into several sections, each with a different length and difficulty level, and it is marked with yellow and black signs. Some of the most famous and popular sections of the trail are: the hike from Kissamos to Elafonisi, which passes through the Balos Lagoon and the Gramvousa Peninsula, the hike from Sougia to Agia Roumeli, which passes through the Agia Irini Gorge and the Omalos Plateau, and the hike from Agios Nikolaos to Sitia, which passes through the Richtis Gorge and the Vai Palm Forest. The trail is open all year round, but it is advisable to avoid the winter months, as some parts can be snowy and dangerous. You also need to wear appropriate shoes and clothing, carry enough water and food, and plan your accommodation and transportation in advance.

WaterSports in Crete

Below are some of the best watersports that you can enjoy in Crete:

Jet Skiing

Jet skiing is one of the most exciting and fun watersports that you can try in Crete. It is a great way to explore the coast, enjoy the scenery, and feel the adrenaline rush. You can rent a jet ski from one of the many watersports centers that are located in the main tourist resorts, such as Hersonissos, Malia, Agios Nikolaos, Rethymnon, and Chania. You can also join a guided jet ski tour, where you can visit some of the most beautiful and secluded spots, such as the Balos Lagoon, the Gramvousa Peninsula, the Spinalonga Island, and the Cretan Caves. Jet skiing is suitable for all ages and skill levels, and you can choose from different models and durations. You need to wear a life jacket and follow the safety rules and instructions of the staff.

Parasailing

Parasailing is another exhilarating and fun watersport that you can try in Crete. It is a great way to enjoy the panoramic views of the sea and the land, and feel the freedom and the breeze. You can parasail from one of the many watersports centers that are located in the main tourist resorts, such as Hersonissos, Malia, Agios Nikolaos, Rethymnon, and Chania. You can also parasail from a boat, where you can take off and land on the deck, and enjoy a scenic cruise along the coast. Parasailing is suitable for all ages and skill levels, and you can choose from different heights and durations. You need to wear a harness and a parachute, and follow the safety rules and instructions of the staff.

Scuba Diving

Scuba diving is one of the most rewarding and fascinating watersports that you can try in Crete. It is a great way to explore the underwater world, discover the marine life, and experience the beauty and the mystery of the sea. You can scuba dive from one of the many diving centers that are located in the main tourist resorts, such as Hersonissos, Malia, Agios Nikolaos, Rethymnon, and Chania. You can also scuba dive from a boat, where you can visit some of the most amazing and diverse dive sites, such as the Dikteon Cave, the Monastery of Kera, the Eco Park, and the Vai Palm Forest. Scuba diving is suitable for all ages and skill levels, and you can choose from different courses and certifications. You need to wear a wetsuit, a mask, a regulator, a buoyancy control device, and fins, and follow the safety rules and instructions of the staff.

Windsurfing

Windsurfing is one of the most challenging and fun watersports that you can try in Crete. It is a great way to enjoy the wind, the waves, and the speed, and feel the thrill and the balance. You can windsurf from one of the many windsurfing centers that are located in the main tourist resorts, such as Hersonissos, Malia, Agios Nikolaos, Rethymnon, and Chania. You can also windsurf from a beach, where you can find the best wind and water conditions, such as the Kouremenos Beach, the Falassarna Beach, the Elafonisi Beach, and the Paleochora Beach. Windsurfing is suitable for all ages and skill levels, and you can choose from different boards and sails. You need to wear a wetsuit, a helmet, a harness, and a life jacket, and follow the safety rules and instructions of the staff.

Kayaking

Kayaking is one of the most relaxing and enjoyable watersports that you can try in Crete. It is a great way to explore the coast, admire the nature, and experience the tranquility and the harmony of the sea. You can kayak from one of the many kayaking centers that are located in the main tourist resorts, such as Hersonissos, Malia, Agios Nikolaos, Rethymnon, and Chania. You can also kayak from a beach, where you can find the best sea and weather conditions, such as the Almyros Beach, the Plakias Beach, the Frangokastello Beach, and the Souda Beach. Kayaking is suitable for all ages and skill levels, and you can choose from different kayaks and paddles. You need to wear a life jacket and follow the safety rules and instructions of the staff.

Horse riding in Crete

Crete is a wonderful destination for horseriding lovers, as it offers a variety of opportunities to enjoy the beauty and the diversity of the island on horseback. Crete has a long tradition of using horses in everyday life, and even today, many Cretans own a Cretan horse, a breed perfectly adapted to the rugged terrains of Crete. Below are some of the best horseriding experiences that you can enjoy in Crete:

Finikia Horseriding

Finikia Horseriding is one of the most popular horseriding centers in Crete, located in the village of Finikia, near Heraklion. The center offers a range of different rides, catering for all levels of riders, from beginners to advanced. You can choose from a variety of options, such as horseriding on the beach, horseriding tours with a wagon and horses on the mountains of Finikia, or horseriding lessons in the arena. The center has a friendly and professional staff, who will guide you through the horseriding process and ensure your safety and comfort. The center also has a collection of well-trained and good-natured horses, suitable for all ages and sizes. Finikia Horseriding is open all year round, from 8:30 am to 9:00 pm, and you need to make a reservation in advance.

Amarillis Stable

Amarillis Stable is another excellent horseriding center in Crete, located in the village of Stalis, near Malia. The center offers a variety of horseriding activities, such as guided trails around the countryside of Stalis, horseriding lessons for adults and children, and horseriding holidays with accommodation and meals. The center has a rustic and elegant setting, with a spacious and airy stable and a lovely and shaded terrace. The center also has a team of experienced and passionate instructors, who will teach you the basics of horseriding or help you improve your skills. The center also has a selection of beautiful and friendly horses, suitable for all levels and ages. Amarillis Stable is open all year round, from 8:30 am to 8:00 pm, and you need to make a reservation in advance.

Zoraida's Horse Riding

Zoraida's Horse Riding is a unique and exclusive horseriding center in Crete, located in the village of Georgioupolis, near Chania. The center offers a variety of horseriding experiences, such as guided trails along the amazing beaches of Georgioupolis, horseriding lessons for beginners and intermediate riders, and horseriding with swimming with horses (weather permitting). The center has a cozy and charming setting, with a wooden and stone stable and a lively and cheerful atmosphere. The center also has a group of professional and enthusiastic guides, who will accompany you through the horseriding adventure and share their knowledge and stories. The center also has a herd of healthy and happy horses, suitable for all levels and ages. Zoraida's Horse Riding is open all year round, from 9:00 am to 7:00 pm, and you need to make a reservation in advance.

Odysseia Stables

Odysseia Stables is a professional and quality horseriding center in Crete, located in the village of

Avdou, near Hersonissos. The center offers a variety of horseriding services, such as guided trails in the surrounding mountainside and the amazing beaches of Hersonissos, horseriding lessons for adults and children, and horseriding holidays with accommodation and activities. The center has a stylish and romantic setting, with a wooden and stone stable and a charming and cozy terrace. The center also has a staff of qualified and passionate instructors, who will train you in the art of horseriding or help you refine your technique. The center also has a collection of elegant and spirited horses, suitable for all levels and ages. Odysseia Stables is open all year round, from 8:30 am to 8:00 pm, and you need to make a reservation in advance.

Kitesurfing in Crete

Below are some of the best kitesurfing spots and schools in Crete:

Kouremenos Beach

Kouremenos Beach is one of the most famous and popular kitesurfing spots in Crete, located in the east of the island, near the town of Sitia. It is a long and sandy beach, with a flat and deep water area, ideal for freeride and freestyle kitesurfing. The wind here is usually strong and steady, blowing from the north-northeast, with an average speed of 15 to 25 knots. The best season to kitesurf here is from May to October, when the wind is more consistent and reliable. Kouremenos Beach is also a great spot for beginners and intermediate kitesurfers, as there are several kitesurfing schools and centers that offer lessons, rentals, and storage. One of them is Kouremenos Surf Club, which has been operating since 1991 and has a team of experienced and certified instructors. Kouremenos Surf Club also has a beach bar, a restaurant, and a shop, where you can relax and enjoy the view.

Elafonisi Beach

Elafonisi Beach is another beautiful and exotic kitesurfing spot in Crete, located in the southwest of the island, near the town of Chania. It is a small and sandy island, connected to the mainland by a shallow and turquoise lagoon, surrounded by pink sand and palm trees. It is a perfect spot for kitesurfing in a tropical and paradisiacal setting, with flat and shallow water, ideal for beginners and freestylers. The wind here is usually moderate and gusty, blowing from the west, with an average speed of 10 to 20 knots. The best season to kitesurf here is from June to September, when the wind is more frequent and stable. Elafonisi Beach is also a popular spot for kitesurfing lessons and tours, as there are several kitesurfing schools and centers that offer them. One of them is Elafonisi Kite, which has been operating since 2010 and has a team of professional and passionate instructors. Elafonisi Kite also has a kite shop, a kite camp, and a kite boat, where you can enjoy the adventure and the scenery.

Falassarna Beach

Falassarna Beach is another amazing and challenging kitesurfing spot in Crete, located in the northwest of the island, near the town of Kissamos. It is a wide and sandy beach, with a choppy and wavy water area, ideal for wave and freeride kitesurfing. The wind here is usually strong and steady, blowing from the northwest, with an average speed of 15 to 25 knots. The best season to kitesurf here is from April to October, when the wind is more consistent and reliable. Falassarna Beach is also a great spot for advanced and experienced kitesurfers, as there are several kitesurfing spots and conditions to choose from, depending on the wind direction and strength. One of them is Falassarna Kite Spot, which is located at the north end of the beach, where the waves are bigger and the wind is stronger. Falassarna Kite Spot also has a kite shop, a kite school, and a kite bar, where you can find everything you need for your kitesurfing session.

Canyoning in Crete

Below are some of the best canyoning experiences that you can enjoy in Crete:

Ha Gorge

Ha Gorge is one of the most impressive and difficult canyons in Crete, located in the east of the island, near the town of Ierapetra. It is the longest gorge in Europe, with a length of 22 km, and it has 27 waterfalls and vertical walls up to 400 m high. The gorge is only suitable for experienced and well-equipped canyoneers, as it requires technical skills, physical strength, and endurance. The descent takes about 10 to 12 hours, depending on the water level and the weather conditions, and it involves hiking, rappelling, swimming, and jumping. Along the way, you will enjoy the spectacular scenery of the gorge, with its towering cliffs, narrow passages, and diverse flora and fauna. You will also pass by the abandoned village of Ha, the Byzantine chapel of Agios Nikolaos, and the famous Iron Gates, the narrowest point of the gorge, where the walls are only 3 m apart. Ha Gorge is open from May to October, and you need to have a permit from the Forest Service of Ierapetra to enter it.

Kalami Gorge

Kalami Gorge is another beautiful and challenging canyon in Crete, located in the south of the island, near the town of Agia Galini. It is a short and steep gorge, with a length of 2 km, and it has several waterfalls and pools. The gorge is suitable for intermediate and advanced canyoneers, as it requires some technical skills, physical fitness, and courage. The descent takes about 3 to 4 hours, depending on the water level and the weather conditions, and it involves hiking, rappelling, swimming, and jumping. Along the way, you will admire the impressive scenery of the gorge, with its rocky walls, shady trees, and colorful flowers. You will also encounter some narrow sections, where the walls are only 2 m apart, and some springs, caves, and ruins. Kalami Gorge is open from May to October, and you need to have a guide or a map to enter it.

Arvi Gorge

Arvi Gorge is a unique and adventurous canyon in Crete, located in the south of the island, near the town of Heraklion. It is a long and dark gorge, with a length of

1.7 km, and it has a 200 m long underground river. The gorge is suitable for experienced and well-equipped canyoneers, as it requires technical skills, physical strength, and mental preparation. The descent takes about 4 to 5 hours, depending on the water level and the weather conditions, and it involves hiking, rappelling, swimming, and crawling. Along the way, you will experience the thrill and the mystery of the gorge, with its pitch-black darkness, cold water, and eerie sounds. You will also pass by an 80 m high waterfall, a stalactite cave, and a bat colony. Arvi Gorge is open from May to October, and you need to have a guide or a map to enter it.

Climbing and Caving in Crete

Below are some of the best climbing and caving experiences that you can enjoy in Crete:

Sport Climbing in Crete

Sport climbing is one of the most popular and accessible forms of climbing, where you can climb on bolted routes with the help of a rope and a partner. Crete has many sport climbing areas, with different types of rock, such as limestone, marble, and conglomerate, and different styles of climbing, such as slabs, overhangs, steep walls, and caves. Some of the most famous and popular sport climbing areas in Crete are:

Kapetaniana: This is the largest and most developed sport climbing area in Crete, located in the south of the island, near the village of Kapetaniana. It has over 130 routes, ranging from 3b to 8a, on solid white limestone rock. The routes are mostly single pitch, but there are also some multi-pitch routes on Mount Kofinas. The area offers a remote and peaceful climbing experience, with stunning views of the sea and the mountains.

Theriso: This is another excellent sport climbing area in Crete, located in the north of the island, near the town of Chania. It has over 40 routes, ranging from 5b to 8a, on various types of rock, such as limestone, marble, and conglomerate. The routes are mostly single pitch, but there are also some multi-pitch routes on the gorge walls. The area offers a diverse and challenging climbing experience, with different styles of climbing, such as slabs, overhangs, and caves.

Plakias: This is a beautiful and exotic sport climbing area in Crete, located in the south of the island, near the town of Rethymnon. It has over 40 routes, ranging from 4c to 8a, on red and gray limestone rock. The routes are mostly single pitch, but there are also some multi-pitch routes on the sea cliffs. The area offers a scenic and adventurous climbing experience, with stunning views of the sea and the palm forest.

Trad Climbing in Crete

Trad climbing is one of the most challenging and rewarding forms of climbing, where you can climb on natural routes with the help of nuts and cams that you place yourself. Crete has many trad climbing areas, with different types of rock, such as limestone, marble, and granite, and different styles of climbing, such as cracks, chimneys, and faces. Some of the most famous and popular trad climbing areas in Crete are:

Mount Gigilos: This is the best trad climbing area in Crete, located in the west of the island, near the famous Samaria Gorge National Park. It has over 20 routes, ranging from VI to VIII+, on solid and compact granite rock. The routes are mostly multi-pitch, ranging from 600m to 1,500m long, and they require a mountaineering approach and a high level of skill and experience. The area offers a spectacular and challenging climbing experience, with breathtaking views of the gorge and the sea.

Marmara: This is a unique and secluded trad climbing area in Crete, located in the south of the island, near the village of Loutro. It has only 5 routes, ranging from 5c to 6b+, on smooth and slippery marble rock. The routes are mostly single pitch, but there is also one multi-pitch route of 100m long. The area offers a tranquil and relaxing climbing experience, with amazing views of the sea and the beach.

Stavros: This is a small and charming trad climbing area in Crete, located in the north of the island, near the town of Chania. It has only 8 routes, ranging from 5b to 6b+, on rough and sharp limestone rock. The routes are mostly multi-pitch, ranging from 50m to 150m long, and they require a moderate level of skill and experience. The area offers a cozy and friendly climbing experience, with lovely views of the bay and the village.

Caving in Crete

Caving is one of the most fascinating and adventurous activities, where you can explore the underground world, discover the geological formations, and experience the beauty and the mystery of the dark. Crete has many caves, with different types of rock, such as limestone, marble, and conglomerate, and different features, such as stalactites, stalagmites, columns, and lakes. Some of the most famous and popular caves in Crete are:

Dikteon Cave: This is one of the most impressive and significant caves in Crete, located in the east of the island, near the town of Agios Nikolaos. It is a large and complex cave, with a length of 2.2 km, and it has many chambers and galleries, decorated with stunning formations. The cave is also known for its archaeological and mythological importance, as it is the birthplace of Zeus, the king of the Greek gods, according to the legend. The cave is open to the public, and you can visit it with a guide or on your own.

Sfentoni Cave: This is another beautiful and interesting cave in Crete, located in the center of the island, near the town of Heraklion. It is a medium-sized and well-preserved cave, with a length of 350 m, and it has one main chamber and several smaller ones, adorned with amazing formations. The cave is also known for its ecological and educational value, as it hosts a variety of fauna and flora, such as bats, spiders, and ferns. The cave is open to the public, and you can visit it with a guide or on your own.

Melidoni Cave: This is a unique and historical cave in Crete, located in the north of the island, near the town of Rethymnon. It is a small and simple cave, with a length of 50 m, and it has one main chamber, with a large opening in the ceiling. The cave is also known for its tragic and heroic history, as it was the site of a massacre and a resistance during the Turkish occupation of Crete. The cave is open to the public, and you can visit it with a guide or on your own.

Wellness: Spas, Retreats, and Yoga

Crete is a wonderful destination for wellness seekers, as it offers a variety of opportunities to relax, rejuvenate, and reconnect with yourself and nature. The island has a natural and holistic approach to wellness, based on the Mediterranean diet, the Cretan lifestyle, and the ancient wisdom of Hippocrates, the father of medicine. Below are some of the best wellness experiences that you can enjoy in Crete:

Spas in Crete

Spas are one of the most popular and accessible forms of wellness, where you can enjoy a range of treatments and services that will enhance your physical and mental well-being. Crete has many spas, with different types of facilities, such as pools, saunas, jacuzzis, and hammams, and different styles of treatments, such as massages, facials, body scrubs, and wraps. Some of the most famous and popular spas in Crete are:

Creta Maris Spa: This is one of the most luxurious and elegant spas in Crete, located in the Creta Maris Beach Resort, near the town of Hersonissos. It has a spacious and modern setting, with a heated indoor pool, a sauna, a steam room, a jacuzzi, and a fitness center. It also has a team of professional and friendly therapists, who will offer you a variety of treatments, such as aromatherapy, reflexology, hot stone massage, and chocolate therapy. Creta Maris Spa also has a beauty salon, where you can enjoy manicures, pedicures, haircuts, and makeup. Creta Maris Spa is open all year round, from 10:00 am to 8:00 pm, and you need to make a reservation in advance.

Ananea Wellness by Aegeo Spas: This is another excellent and quality spa in Crete, located in the Anemos Luxury Grand Resort, near the town of Chania. It has a cozy and charming setting, with a heated indoor pool, a sauna, a steam room, a jacuzzi, and a relaxation area. It also has a staff of experienced and passionate therapists, who will offer you a variety of treatments, such as Swedish massage, deep tissue massage, facial massage, and body peeling. Ananea Wellness by Aegeo Spas also has a fitness center, where you can work out and stay in shape. Ananea Wellness by Aegeo Spas is open all year round, from 10:00 am to 8:00 pm, and you need to make a reservation in advance.

Thalasso by Aegeo Spas: This is a unique and exclusive spa in Crete, located in the Cavo Spada Luxury Resort & Spa, near the town of Chania. It is a thalassotherapy center, which uses seawater and marine products to provide health and beauty benefits. It has a large and impressive setting, with a seawater pool, a sauna, a steam room, a jacuzzi, and a fitness center. It also has a team of qualified and dedicated therapists, who will offer you a variety of treatments, such as seaweed wrap, marine mud wrap, hydro massage, and jet shower. Thalasso by Aegeo Spas also has a beauty salon, where you can enjoy manicures, pedicures, haircuts, and makeup. Thalasso by Aegeo Spas is open all year round, from 10:00 am to 8:00 pm, and you need to make a reservation in advance.

Retreats in Crete

Retreats are one of the most rewarding and transformative forms of wellness, where you can escape from the stress and noise of everyday life, and focus on your personal growth and development. Crete has many retreats, with different types of themes, such as meditation, yoga, detox, healing, and spirituality, and different styles of accommodation, such as hotels, villas, cottages, and camps. Some of the most famous and popular retreats in Crete are:

Cretan Yoga Retreat: This is one of the most relaxing and enjoyable retreats in Crete, located in the village of Agios Pavlos, near the town of Rethymnon. It is a yoga retreat, where you can practice various types of yoga, such as hatha, vinyasa, yin, and restorative, with the guidance of experienced and certified instructors. You can also enjoy other activities, such as meditation, pranayama, chanting, and dancing, as well as excursions, such as hiking, swimming, and sightseeing. The retreat offers comfortable and cozy accommodation, in a traditional stone house, with a stunning view of the sea and the mountains. The retreat also offers delicious and healthy vegetarian meals, prepared with fresh and organic ingredients. The retreat is open from April to October, and you can choose from different durations and packages.

Cretan Detox Retreat: This is another excellent and quality retreat in Crete, located in the village of Kamilari, near the town of Heraklion. It is a detox retreat, where you can cleanse your body and mind, and boost your energy and vitality. You can also enjoy other activities, such as yoga, pilates, massage, and acupuncture, with the support of professional and friendly staff. The retreat offers luxurious and spacious accommodation, in a modern and elegant villa, with a private pool and a garden. The retreat also offers nutritious and tasty vegan meals, prepared with fresh and organic ingredients. The retreat is open all year round, and you can choose from different durations and packages.

Cretan Healing Retreat: This is a unique and special retreat in Crete, located in the village of Zaros, near the town of Heraklion. It is a healing retreat, where you can heal your physical and emotional wounds, and restore your balance and harmony. You can also enjoy other activities, such as meditation, reiki, sound healing, and art therapy, with the guidance of skilled and compassionate therapists. The retreat offers simple and cozy accommodation, in a traditional and rustic cottage, with a beautiful view of the lake and the forest. The retreat also offers wholesome and organic meals, prepared with local and seasonal ingredients. The retreat is open all year round, and you can choose from different durations and packages.

Yoga in Crete

Yoga is one of the most popular and beneficial forms of

wellness, where you can improve your physical and mental health, and enhance your flexibility and strength. Crete has many yoga options, with different types of yoga, such as hatha, vinyasa, yin, and restorative, and different styles of settings, such as studios, beaches, and mountains. Some of the best yoga options in Crete are:

Yoga Rocks: This is one of the most scenic and serene yoga options in Crete, located in the village of Triopetra, near the town of Rethymnon. It is a yoga studio, where you can practice various types of yoga, such as hatha, vinyasa, yin, and restorative, with the guidance of experienced and certified instructors. You can also enjoy other activities, such as meditation, pranayama, chanting, and dancing, as well as excursions, such as hiking, swimming, and sightseeing. The studio offers comfortable and cozy accommodation, in a traditional stone house, with a stunning view of the sea and the mountains. The studio also offers delicious and healthy vegetarian meals, prepared with fresh and organic ingredients. The studio is open from April to October, and you can choose from different durations and packages.

Yoga Plus: This is another excellent and quality yoga option in Crete, located in the village of Agios Pavlos, near the town of Rethymnon. It is a yoga studio, where you can practice various types of yoga, such as hatha, vinyasa, yin, and restorative, with the guidance of experienced and certified instructors. You can also enjoy other activities, such as meditation, pranayama, chanting, and dancing, as well as excursions, such as hiking, swimming, and sightseeing. The studio offers luxurious and spacious accommodation, in a modern and elegant villa, with a private pool and a garden. The studio also offers nutritious and tasty vegan meals, prepared with fresh and organic ingredients. The studio is open from April to October, and you can choose from different durations and packages.

Yoga on Crete: This is a unique and flexible yoga option in Crete, located in the village of Sfakia, near the town of Chania. It is a yoga service, where you can practice various types of yoga, such as hatha, vinyasa, yin, and restorative, with the guidance of experienced and certified instructors. You can also enjoy other activities, such as meditation, pranayama, chanting, and dancing, as well as excursions, such as hiking, swimming, and sightseeing. The service offers different types of accommodation, such as hotels, villas, cottages, and camps, depending on your preferences and budget.

The service also offers different types of meals, such as vegetarian, vegan, gluten-free, and raw, depending on your preferences and needs. The service is open all year round, and you can choose from different durations and packages.

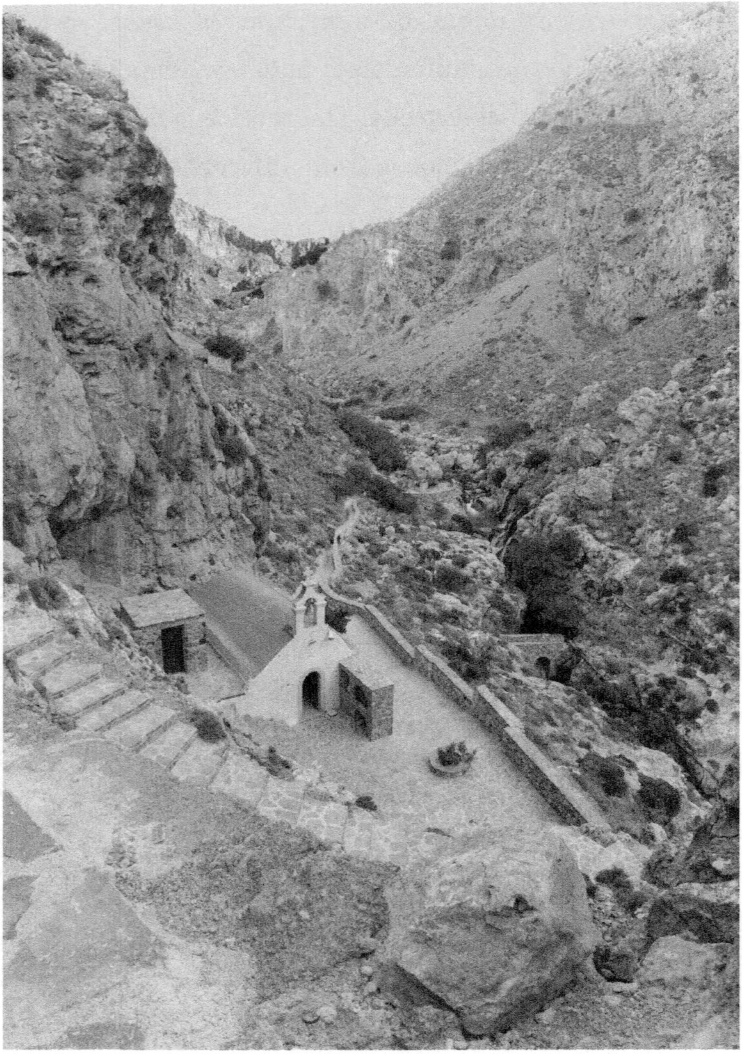

Chapter 9 • Shopping in Crete

Fashion and Luxury Shopping

Below are some of the best fashion and luxury shopping experiences that you can enjoy in Crete:

Shopping Malls in Crete

Shopping malls are one of the most popular and convenient forms of shopping, where you can find a range of stores and services under one roof. Crete has many shopping malls, with different types of facilities, such as cinemas, restaurants, cafes, and playgrounds, and different styles of stores, such as fashion, beauty, electronics, and home. Some of the most famous and popular shopping malls in Crete are:

Talos Plaza: This is one of the largest and most modern shopping malls in Crete, located in the city of Heraklion. It has over 70 stores, offering a variety of products, such as clothing, shoes, bags, jewelry, watches, cosmetics, perfumes, books, toys, and gadgets. It also has a cinema, a food court, a coffee shop, and a supermarket. Talos Plaza is open all year round, from 9:00 am to 9:00 pm, and it has free parking and free

Wi-Fi.

ANEK Lines: This is another excellent and quality shopping mall in Crete, located in the city of Chania. It is a part of the ANEK Lines ferry company, and it offers a unique and exclusive shopping experience on board. It has over 20 stores, offering a variety of products, such as clothing, shoes, bags, jewelry, watches, cosmetics, perfumes, books, toys, and gadgets. It also has a restaurant, a bar, and a casino. ANEK Lines is open all year round, from 7:00 am to 11:00 pm, and it has free parking and free Wi-Fi.

Fashion Boutiques in Crete

Some of the most famous and popular fashion boutiques in Crete are:

Candiashop Boutique: This is one of the most chic and cozy fashion boutiques in Crete, located in the city of Heraklion. It specializes in plus size clothing, offering a variety of products, such as dresses, skirts, pants, tops, jackets, and coats. It also offers a variety of accessories, such as bags, scarves, hats, and belts. Candiashop Boutique is open all year round, from 10:00 am to 9:00 pm, and it has a friendly and helpful staff.

Zalo: This is another excellent and quality fashion boutique in Crete, located in the city of Chania. It specializes in leather goods, offering a variety of products, such as shoes, boots, sandals, bags, wallets, belts, and gloves. It also offers a variety of accessories, such as jewelry, sunglasses, hats, and umbrellas. Zalo is open all year round, from 9:00 am to 9:00 pm, and it has a professional and knowledgeable staff.

Jewelry and Watch Shops in Crete

Some of the most famous and popular jewelry and watch shops in Crete are:

Sifis Stavroulakis: This is one of the most impressive and prestigious jewelry and watch shops in Crete, located in the city of Heraklion. It offers a variety of products, such as rings, earrings, necklaces, bracelets, pendants, and brooches, made of gold, silver, platinum, and precious stones. It also offers a variety of products, such as watches, clocks, and pens, made of stainless steel, titanium, and leather. It also offers a variety of services, such as engraving, repairing, and appraising. Sifis Stavroulakis is open all year round, from 9:00 am to 9:00 pm, and it has a courteous and experienced staff.

Pod - Paint On Demand: This is another unique and creative jewelry and watch shop in Crete, located in the city of Chania. It offers a variety of products, such as rings, earrings, necklaces, bracelets, pendants, and brooches, made of silver, bronze, copper, and resin. It also offers a variety of products, such as watches, clocks, and pens, made of wood, metal, and plastic. It also offers a variety of services, such as customizing, painting, and designing. Pod - Paint On Demand is open all year round, from 10:00 am to 9:00 pm, and it has a friendly and passionate staff.

Art and Souvenir Shops in Crete

Art and souvenir shops are one of the most interesting and enjoyable forms of shopping, where you can find a range of products that will reflect your memories and experiences of the island. Crete has many art and souvenir shops, with different types of products, such as paintings, sculptures, ceramics, textiles, and magnets, and different styles of products, such as traditional and contemporary, realistic and abstract, and colorful and monochrome. Some of the most famous and popular art and souvenir shops in Crete are:

Botano: This is one of the most natural and authentic art and souvenir shops in Crete, located in the village of Kouses, near the town of Heraklion. It offers a variety of products, such as herbs, spices, teas, oils, honeys, and soaps, made of organic and local ingredients. It also offers a variety of products, such as candles, incense, books, and music, made of natural and eco-friendly materials. It also offers a variety of services, such as workshops, tours, and tastings. Botano is open all year round, from 9:00 am to 9:00 pm, and it has a warm and welcoming staff.

Omen Art Gallery-Art Shop: This is another excellent and quality art and souvenir shop in Crete, located in the city of Rethymnon. It offers a variety of products, such as paintings, sculptures, ceramics, glass, and wood, made by local and international artists. It also offers a variety of products, such as jewelry, bags, scarves, and hats, made by local and international designers. It also offers a variety of services, such as framing, shipping, and consulting. Omen Art Gallery-Art Shop is open all year round, from 10:00 am to 9:00 pm, and it has a professional and friendly staff.

Tophane: This is another unique and exclusive art and antique market in Crete, located in the city of Chania. It is a historic and picturesque district, with a mix of Venetian and Ottoman buildings, and a bohemian vibe. It has over 10 shops, offering a variety of products, such as paintings, sculptures, icons, furniture, and coins, made by local and international artists and collectors. It also has several cafes and bars, where you can relax and enjoy the view. Tophane is open all year round, from 9:00 am to 9:00 pm, and it has a cozy and charming atmosphere.

Local Markets and Souvenirs

Below are some of the best local markets and souvenirs that you can enjoy in Crete:

Food and Drink Markets in Crete

Food and drink markets are one of the most popular and delicious forms of shopping, where you can find a range of products that will tantalize your taste buds and satisfy your appetite. Crete has many food and drink markets, with different types of products, such as fruits and vegetables, cheese and yogurt, olive oil and olives, honey and herbs, wine and raki, and pastries and sweets. Some of the most famous and popular food and drink markets in Crete are:

Old Chania Market: This is one of the most impressive and historic food and drink markets in Crete, located in the city of Chania. It is a large and covered market, built in 1913, with a cross-shaped layout and a neoclassical style. It has over 70 stalls, offering a variety of products, such as cheese, meat, fish, bread, spices, nuts, and souvenirs. It also has several cafes and taverns, where you can enjoy a coffee or a meal. Old Chania Market is open all year round, from 8:00 am to 8:00 pm, and it has a lively and colorful atmosphere.

Heraklion Central Market: This is another excellent and bustling food and drink market in Crete, located in the city of Heraklion. It is a long and narrow street market, stretching for about 1 km, with a mix of modern and traditional shops. It has over 100 stalls, offering a variety of products, such as fruits, vegetables, cheese, meat, fish, olives, honey, herbs, and souvenirs. It also has several cafes and taverns, where you can enjoy a drink or a snack. Heraklion Central Market is open all year round, from 7:00 am to 3:00 pm, and it has a friendly and lively atmosphere.

Clothing and Accessory Markets in Crete

Some of the most famous and popular clothing and accessory markets in Crete are:

Skrydlof Street: This is one of the most chic and cozy clothing and accessory markets in Crete, located in the city of Chania. It is a short and narrow street, with a mix of old and new buildings, and a bohemian vibe. It has over 20 shops, offering a variety of products, such as leather goods, knitwear, embroidery, and souvenirs. It also has several cafes and bars, where you can relax and enjoy the view. Skrydlof Street is open all year round, from 9:00 am to 9:00 pm, and it has a warm and welcoming atmosphere.

Market Center - Skaleta: This is another excellent and quality clothing and accessory market in Crete, located in the village of Skaleta, near the town of Rethymnon. It is a large and modern market, with a spacious and airy layout and a variety of facilities. It has over 50 shops, offering a variety of products, such as clothing, shoes, bags, jewelry, and souvenirs. It also has a cinema, a restaurant, a cafe, and a playground. Market Center - Skaleta is open all year round, from 9:00 am to 9:00 pm, and it has a friendly and professional staff.

Pottery and Ceramic Markets in Crete

Some of the most famous and popular pottery and ceramic markets in Crete are:

Margarites: This is one of the most impressive and authentic pottery and ceramic markets in Crete, located in the village of Margarites, near the town of Rethymnon. It is a small and picturesque village, with a long history and a rich culture of pottery making. It has over 20 workshops, offering a variety of products, such as earthenware, stoneware, and porcelain. You can also watch the potters at work, learn about the techniques and the materials, and even try your hand at pottery making. Margarites is open all year round, from 9:00 am to 9:00 pm, and it has a charming and rustic atmosphere.

Thrapsano: This is another excellent and quality pottery and ceramic market in Crete, located in the village of Thrapsano, near the town of Heraklion. It is a large and lively village, with a strong tradition and a high reputation of pottery making. It has over 30 workshops, offering a variety of products, such as pots, jars, amphorae, and tiles. You can also watch the potters at work, learn about the history and the symbolism of pottery, and even participate in pottery festivals and events. Thrapsano is open all year round, from 9:00 am to 9:00 pm, and it has a friendly and festive atmosphere.

Artisan Crafts and Workshops

Below are some of the best artisan crafts and workshop experiences that you can enjoy in Crete:

Pottery and Ceramics in Crete

Pottery and ceramics are one of the most ancient and characteristic forms of artisan crafts in Crete, dating back to the Minoan civilization. The island has a long and rich tradition of pottery making, using clay, water, fire, and various tools and techniques to create functional and decorative objects, such as pots, plates, cups, vases, and figurines. The island also has a variety of styles and colors of pottery and ceramics, influenced by different cultures and periods, such as geometric, floral, animal, and human motifs, and red, black, white, and blue hues. One of the best pottery and ceramics experience in Crete are:

Pottery Workshop and Folk Arts Tour in Chania: This is an excellent and quality pottery and ceramics tour in Crete. It is a full-day tour, starting from the city of Chania, and visiting various places related to pottery and folk arts, such as the Historical and Folklore Museum of Theriso, the Pottery Workshop of Vassilis Politakis, and the Botanical Park and Gardens of Crete. You can also enjoy a pottery lesson, a pottery demonstration, a pottery exhibition, and a pottery souvenir. The tour also includes a traditional lunch, a wine tasting, and a honey tasting. The tour is available from April to October, and it costs 120 euros per person.

Weaving and Embroidery in Crete

Weaving and embroidery are another ancient and characteristic forms of artisan crafts in Crete, dating back to the Minoan civilization. The island has a long and rich tradition of weaving and embroidery, using wool, cotton, silk, and linen, and various looms and needles, to create functional and decorative objects, such as rugs, blankets, curtains, tablecloths, and clothes. The island also has a variety of styles and patterns of weaving and embroidery, influenced by different regions and periods, such as geometric, floral, animal, and human motifs, and red, blue, green, and yellow colors. Some of the best weaving and embroidery experiences in Crete are:

Anogia: This is one of the most famous and traditional weaving and embroidery villages in Crete, located in the Rethymnon region. It is a large and lively village, with a strong identity and a high reputation of weaving and embroidery. It has over 10 workshops, offering a variety of products, such as rugs, blankets, curtains, tablecloths, and clothes. You can also watch the weavers and embroiderers at work, learn about the techniques and the materials, and even try your hand at weaving and embroidery. Anogia is open all year round, from 9:00 am to 9:00 pm, and it has a friendly and festive atmosphere.

Weaving and Embroidery Workshop in Heraklion: This is a unique and creative weaving and embroidery workshop in Crete. It is a half-day workshop, starting from the city of Heraklion, and visiting the workshop of Maria Sanoudaki, a renowned weaver and embroiderer. You can also enjoy a weaving and embroidery lesson, a weaving and embroidery demonstration, a weaving and embroidery exhibition, and a weaving and embroidery souvenir. The workshop also includes a coffee break, a snack, and a drink. The workshop is available from May to October, and it costs 65 euros per person.

Leather and Woodwork in Crete

One of the best leather and woodwork experience in Crete are:

Leather and Woodwork Workshop in Rethymnon: This is an excellent and quality leather and woodwork workshop in Crete. It is a full-day workshop, starting from the city of Rethymnon, and visiting the workshop of Giorgos and Kostas, two brothers who are experts in leather and woodwork. You can also enjoy a leather and woodwork lesson, a leather and woodwork demonstration, a leather and woodwork exhibition, and a leather and woodwork souvenir. The workshop also includes a traditional lunch, a wine tasting, and a cheese tasting. The workshop is available from May to October, and it costs 120 euros per person.

Jewelry and Metalwork in Crete

One of the best jewelry and metalwork experiences in Crete are:

Jewelry and Metalwork Workshop in Chania: This is a unique and exclusive jewelry and metalwork workshop in Crete. It is a half-day workshop, starting from the city of Chania, and visiting the workshop of Yannis Kelesis, a renowned jeweler and metalworker. You can also enjoy a jewelry and metalwork lesson, a jewelry and metalwork demonstration, a jewelry and metalwork exhibition, and a jewelry and metalwork souvenir. The workshop also includes a coffee break, a snack, and a drink. The workshop is available from May to October, and it costs 75 euros per person.

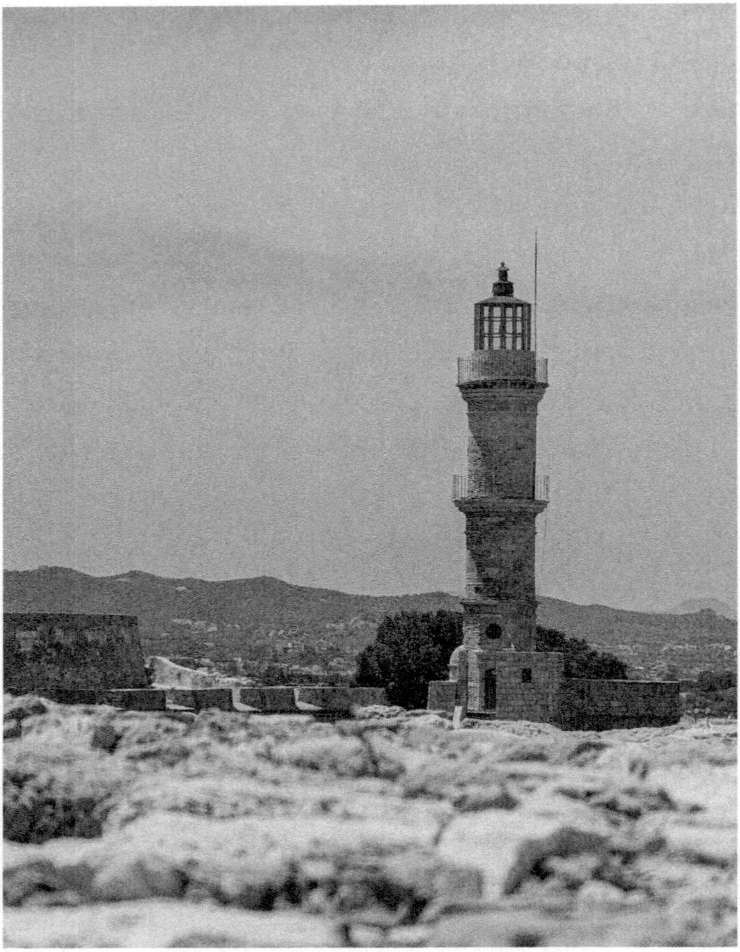

Chapter 10 • Practical Information

Health and Safety Tips

Crete is safe and healthy for travelers, as it has a low crime rate, a high-quality health care system, and a natural and holistic approach to wellness. However, as with any travel destination, there are some risks and precautions that you should be aware of and follow to ensure a smooth and enjoyable trip. Below are some of the most important health and safety tips that you should know before and during your visit to Crete:

Travel insurance: It is highly recommended that you purchase a comprehensive travel insurance policy that covers medical expenses, repatriation, cancellation, theft, and other emergencies. Although Crete has a public health care system that is free or low-cost for EU citizens, you may still need to pay for some services or medications, or seek private treatment. Having travel insurance will give you peace of mind and save you from potential financial troubles.

Vaccinations: There are no specific vaccinations required for traveling to Crete, but it is advisable that you are up to date with your routine vaccinations, such as tetanus, diphtheria, polio, measles, mumps, and rubella. You may also consider getting vaccinated for hepatitis A and B, typhoid, and rabies, depending on your travel plans and activities. You should consult your doctor or a travel clinic at least six weeks before your departure to get the appropriate advice and shots.

Sun protection: Crete has a sunny and warm climate, especially from May to October, when the temperatures can reach up to 40°C. While this is great for enjoying the beaches and the outdoors, it also poses a risk of sunburn, heatstroke, and dehydration. You should protect yourself from the sun by wearing a hat, sunglasses, and sunscreen with a high SPF, and by avoiding exposure during the hottest hours of the day (11:00 am to 4:00 pm). You should also drink plenty of water and avoid alcohol and caffeine, which can dehydrate you further.

Water quality: Tap water in Crete is generally safe to drink, but it may have a different taste or mineral content than what you are used to. If you have a sensitive stomach or prefer a better taste, you can buy bottled water, which is widely available and inexpensive. You should also avoid drinking water from streams, wells, or fountains, unless they are clearly marked as potable, as they may be contaminated by bacteria or parasites.

Food safety: Food in Crete is delicious and healthy, based on the Mediterranean diet, which includes fresh fruits and vegetables, olive oil, cheese, yogurt, fish, and meat. However, you should still be careful about what and where you eat, as you may encounter some foodborne illnesses, such as diarrhea, salmonella, or E. coli. You should avoid eating raw or undercooked meat, eggs, or seafood, unpasteurized dairy products, or unwashed fruits and vegetables. You should also choose clean and reputable restaurants, cafes, or street vendors, and avoid eating leftovers or food that has been left out for a long time.

Driving safety: Driving in Crete can be a convenient and enjoyable way to explore the island, but it can also be challenging and risky, especially for inexperienced or foreign drivers. The roads in Crete are often narrow, winding, steep, and poorly maintained, and the traffic can be chaotic, fast, and aggressive. You should drive with caution and respect the local rules and customs, such as using your horn, giving way to the right, and overtaking on the left. You should also have a valid driver's license, an international driving permit, a car insurance, and a road map or a GPS. You should avoid driving at night, in bad weather, or under the influence of alcohol or drugs.

Crime and scams: Crete is a relatively safe destination, with a low crime rate and a friendly and hospitable population. However, you should still be aware of some common crimes and scams that may target tourists, such as pickpocketing, bag snatching, car theft, or overcharging. You should keep your valuables and documents in a safe place, such as a hotel safe or a money belt, and avoid carrying large amounts of cash or flashy items. You should also be careful of strangers who may approach you with offers, requests, or distractions, and always check the prices and receipts before paying for anything.

Emergency Contacts

Crete is a safe and beautiful destination for travelers, but sometimes emergencies can happen, and you may need to contact the local authorities or services for help.

General Emergency Number: 112

The general emergency number in Crete, as well as in the rest of Greece and the European Union, is 112. You can call this number from any phone, even without a SIM card, and it is free of charge. You can use this number to reach any emergency service, such as the police, the fire brigade, or the ambulance, depending on your situation. When you call 112, you will be asked to provide your name, location, and the type of emergency. You can also request an operator who speaks English or another language, if you do not speak Greek. The operator will then connect you to the appropriate service or provide you with the necessary information and instructions. You should call 112 only in case of a serious emergency, and not for minor or non-urgent issues.

Police: 100

The police number in Crete, as well as in the rest of Greece, is 100. You can call this number from any phone, and it is free of charge. You can use this number to report a crime, an accident, or a disturbance, or to request assistance or protection. When you call 100, you will be connected to the nearest police station, and you will be asked to provide your name, location, and the reason for your call. You can also request an operator who speaks English or another language, if you do not speak Greek. The police will then send a patrol car or an officer to your location, or provide you with the necessary information and instructions. You should call 100 only in case of a serious or urgent issue, and not for minor or non-urgent issues.

Fire Brigade: 199

The fire brigade number in Crete, as well as in the rest of Greece, is 199. You can call this number from any phone, and it is free of charge. You can use this number to report a fire, an explosion, or a rescue, or to request assistance or prevention. When you call 199, you will be connected to the nearest fire station, and you will be asked to provide your name, location, and the type of emergency. You can also request an operator who speaks English or another language, if you do not speak Greek. The fire brigade will then send a fire truck or a rescue team to your location, or provide you with the necessary information and instructions. You should call 199 only in case of a serious or urgent issue, and not for minor or non-urgent issues.

Ambulance: 166

The ambulance number in Crete, as well as in the rest of Greece, is 166. You can call this number from any phone, and it is free of charge. You can use this number to request urgent medical assistance or transportation to a hospital, or to report a medical emergency. When you call 166, you will be connected to the National Center for Emergency Care (EKAB), and you will be asked to provide your name, location, and the type of emergency. You can also request an operator who speaks English or another language, if you do not speak Greek. The ambulance will then send a paramedic or a doctor to your location, or provide you with the necessary information and instructions. You should call 166 only in case of a serious or urgent issue, and not for minor or non-urgent issues.

Coast Guard: 108

The coast guard number in Crete, as well as in the rest of Greece, is 108. You can call this number from any phone, and it is free of charge. You can use this number to report a maritime emergency, such as a shipwreck, a drowning, or a pollution, or to request assistance or information. When you call 108, you will be connected to the nearest coast guard station, and you will be asked to provide your name, location, and the type of emergency. You can also request an operator who speaks English or another language, if you do not speak Greek. The coast guard will then send a patrol boat or a helicopter to your location, or provide you with the necessary information and instructions. You should call

108 only in case of a serious or urgent issue, and not for minor or non-urgent issues.

Hospitals in Crete

Crete has a public health care system that is free or low-cost for EU citizens, and a private health care system that is more expensive but may offer better quality or faster service. You can choose to visit a public or a private hospital, depending on your preference, budget, and insurance. You can also visit a health center or a clinic, which are smaller and less equipped than hospitals, but may be closer or more convenient. Below are some of the most popular hospitals in Crete, both public and private:

General Hospital St. George: This is one of the largest and most modern public hospitals in Crete, located in the city of Chania1. It has over 500 beds, and it offers a variety of services, such as emergency, surgery, cardiology, neurology, oncology, and pediatrics. It also has a helipad, a blood bank, and a pharmacy. It is open 24/7, and you can contact it at +30 2821 342000.

Venizeleio General Hospital: This is another excellent and quality public hospital in Crete, located in the city of Heraklion. It has over 400 beds, and it offers a variety of services, such as emergency, surgery, cardiology, neurology, oncology, and pediatrics. It also has a helipad, a blood bank, and a pharmacy. It is open 24/7, and you can contact it at +30 2813 408000.

Iasis Hospital: This is one of the most impressive and prestigious private hospitals in Crete, located in the city of Heraklion. It has over 200 beds, and it offers a variety of services, such as emergency, surgery, cardiology, neurology, oncology, and pediatrics. It also has a helipad, a blood bank, and a pharmacy. It is open 24/7, and you can contact it at +30 2810 370000.

Agios Nikolaos General Hospital: This is another excellent and quality private hospital in Crete, located in the city of Agios Nikolaos. It has over 100 beds, and it offers a variety of services, such as emergency, surgery, cardiology, neurology, oncology, and pediatrics. It also has a helipad, a blood bank, and a pharmacy. It is open 24/7, and you can contact it at +30 2841 340000.

Communication and Internet Access

Below are some of the most important communication and internet access tips that you should know before and during your visit to Crete:

Phone Calls in Crete

Phone calls are one of the most common and convenient forms of communication, where you can talk to your family, friends, or business partners, or get information or assistance. Crete has a dual phone system, with both landline and mobile phones, and different types of phone numbers, such as local, national, international, and toll-free. Below are some of the most important phone call tips that you should know in Crete:

Landline Phones: Landline phones are the fixed phones that are connected to a wall socket, and they are usually found in hotels, offices, or public places. Landline phone numbers in Crete have 10 digits, starting with the area code 282, 283, or 284, followed by the local number. For example, the landline phone number of the General Hospital St. George in Chania is +30 2821 342000. To make a landline phone call in Crete, you can use a landline phone, a mobile phone, or a phone card. You can also use a public phone booth, which are located in most streets and squares, and accept coins or phone cards. Phone cards can be bought from kiosks, post offices, or phone shops, and they have different values, such as 5, 10, or 20 euros. To make a local landline phone call in Crete, you just need to dial the 10-digit number. To make a national landline phone call in

Crete, you need to dial 0 followed by the 10-digit number. To make an international landline phone call in Crete, you need to dial 00 followed by the country code, the area code, and the local number.

Mobile Phones: Mobile phones are the portable phones that are connected to a wireless network, and they are usually owned by individuals or companies. Mobile phone numbers in Crete have 10 digits, starting with the network code 69, followed by the personal number. For example, the mobile phone number of the tourist police in Chania is +30 6972 774466. To make a mobile phone call in Crete, you can use a mobile phone, a landline phone, or a phone card. You can also use a public phone booth, which are located in some streets and squares, and accept coins or phone cards. To make a local mobile phone call in Crete, you just need to dial the 10-digit number. To make a national mobile phone call in Crete, you need to dial 0 followed by the 10-digit number. To make an international mobile phone call in Crete, you need to dial 00 followed by the country code, the network code, and the personal number.

Phone Charges: Phone charges are the fees that you have to pay for making or receiving phone calls, and they depend on various factors, such as the type of phone, the type of number, the duration of the call, the time of the day, and the provider. Generally, landline phone calls are cheaper than mobile phone calls, local phone calls are cheaper than national or international phone calls, and off-peak phone calls are cheaper than peak phone calls. Phone charges are usually included in your phone bill, which you can pay online, by phone, or at a bank, a post office, or a phone shop. If you use a phone card, you can check the remaining balance by dialing 121. If you use a public phone booth, you can see the cost of the call on the display.

Internet Access in Crete

Internet access is one of the most useful forms of communication, where you can access various online services and platforms, such as email, social media, web browsing, streaming, or gaming. Crete has a high-speed and low-cost internet service, with a wide coverage of broadband and wireless networks, and a variety of devices and plans. Below are some of the most important internet access tips that you should know in Crete:

Broadband Internet: Broadband internet is the fixed internet service that is connected to a wall socket, and it is usually found in hotels, offices, or homes. Broadband internet in Crete has a speed of up to 100 Mbps, and it is provided by various providers, such as Otenet, Forthnet, Vodafone, or Wind. To use broadband internet in Crete, you need to have a modem, a router, and a cable, and you need to subscribe to a plan that suits your needs and budget. You can also use a laptop, a tablet, or a smartphone, and you need to connect to the Wi-Fi network and enter the password. To subscribe to a broadband internet plan in Crete, you need to visit a provider's website, a phone shop, or a kiosk, and you need to provide your personal details, your address, and your payment method. You can also choose from different plans, such as monthly, yearly, or prepaid, and different speeds, such as 24, 50, or 100 Mbps. Broadband internet charges are usually included in your phone bill, which you can pay online, by phone, or at a bank, a post office, or a phone shop.

Wireless Internet: Wireless internet is the portable internet service that is connected to a wireless network, and it is usually found in public places, such as cafes, restaurants, bars, or parks. Wireless internet in Crete has a speed of up to 50 Mbps, and it is provided by various providers, such as Cosmote, Vodafone, or Wind. To use wireless internet in Crete, you need to have a device, such as a laptop, a tablet, or a smartphone, and you need to connect to the Wi-Fi network and enter the password. To access a wireless internet network in Crete, you need to visit a public place that offers free Wi-Fi, such as a cafe, a restaurant, a bar, or a park, and you need to ask for the password or scan a QR code. You can also use a hotspot device, such as a dongle, a MiFi, or a mobile phone, and you need to buy a SIM card or a data plan that suits your needs and budget. You can also use a public hotspot network, such as Fon, and you need to register and pay a fee. Wireless internet charges are usually included in your data plan, which you can buy online, by phone, or at a kiosk, or in your hotspot fee, which you can pay online, by phone, or at a bank, a post office, or a phone shop.

Chapter 11 • Recommended Itineraries

One day in Crete

Crete is a large and diverse island, with many attractions and activities to suit every taste and interest. However, if you only have one day to explore Crete, you can still enjoy some of the highlights and get a glimpse of the beauty and culture of the island. Below is a suggested itinerary for one day in Crete, based on the most popular and convenient destinations and experiences:

Start your day in Chania, one of the most charming and historic cities in Crete. Wander around the picturesque old town, admire the Venetian and Ottoman architecture, and visit the impressive Venetian harbor and the lighthouse. You can also visit the Archaeological Museum, the Maritime Museum, or the Folklore Museum, to learn more about the history and the traditions of Crete.

Next, drive to Elafonisi, one of the most stunning and exotic beaches in Crete. Enjoy the crystal clear water, the soft white and pink sand, and the natural beauty of the lagoon and the island. You can also explore the nearby cedar forest, the sand dunes, and the rock formations, or visit the Agia Irini Monastery and the Chrysoskalitissa Monastery, to see some of the religious and historical sites of the area.

Then, drive to Balos, another spectacular and scenic beach in Crete. Take a boat from Kissamos or drive to the parking lot and hike to the beach, and marvel at the turquoise water, the white sand, and the rocky islet of Gramvousa. You can also swim, snorkel, or sunbathe, or visit the Gramvousa Castle and the Balos Lagoon, to see some of the natural and cultural attractions of the area.

Finally, drive back to Chania, and enjoy the nightlife and the cuisine of the city. You can choose from a variety of bars, clubs, and restaurants, offering local and international music, drinks, and food. You can also sample some of the traditional dishes and specialties of Crete, such as dakos, kalitsounia, boureki, or raki, and experience the hospitality and the atmosphere of the island.

Three days in Crete

Below is a suggested itinerary for three days in Crete, based on the most popular and convenient destinations and experiences:

Day 1: Chania and Elafonisi

Start your day in Chania, one of the most charming and historic cities in Crete. Wander around the picturesque old town, admire the Venetian and Ottoman architecture, and visit the impressive Venetian harbor and the lighthouse. You can also visit the Archaeological Museum, the Maritime Museum, or the Folklore Museum, to learn more about the history and the traditions of Crete.

Next, drive to Elafonisi, one of the most stunning and exotic beaches in Crete. Enjoy the crystal clear water, the soft white and pink sand, and the natural beauty of the lagoon and the island. You can also explore the nearby cedar forest, the sand dunes, and the rock formations, or visit the Agia Irini Monastery and the Chrysoskalitissa Monastery, to see some of the religious and historical sites of the area.

Day 2: Rethymnon and Balos

Start your day in Rethymnon, one of the most elegant and lively cities in Crete. Explore the beautiful old town, admire the Venetian and Ottoman architecture, and visit the majestic Fortezza and the Rimondi Fountain. You can also visit the Archaeological Museum, the Historical and Folklore Museum, or the Centre of Contemporary

Art, to learn more about the history and the culture of Crete.

Next, drive to Balos, another spectacular and scenic beach in Crete. Take a boat from Kissamos or drive to the parking lot and hike to the beach, and marvel at the turquoise water, the white sand, and the rocky islet of Gramvousa. You can also swim, snorkel, or sunbathe, or visit the Gramvousa Castle and the Balos Lagoon, to see some of the natural and cultural attractions of the area.

Day 3: Heraklion and Knossos

Start your day in Heraklion, one of the most modern and vibrant cities in Crete. Visit the impressive Venetian fortress and the port, and stroll along the pedestrian street of 25th August. You can also visit the Archaeological Museum, the Historical Museum, or the Natural History Museum, to learn more about the history and the nature of Crete.

Next, drive to Knossos, one of the most famous and fascinating archaeological sites in Crete. Explore the ancient palace of the Minoans, the oldest civilization in Europe, and admire the colorful frescoes, the intricate architecture, and the mysterious legends. You can also visit the nearby Archaeological Site of Malia, another important Minoan palace, or the Archaeological Site of

Phaistos, another impressive Minoan settlement

Five days in Crete

Below is a suggested itinerary for five days in Crete, based on the most popular and convenient destinations and experiences:

Day 1: Chania and Elafonisi

Start your day in Chania, one of the most charming and historic cities in Crete. Wander around the picturesque old town, admire the Venetian and Ottoman architecture, and visit the impressive Venetian harbor and the lighthouse. You can also visit the Archaeological Museum, the Maritime Museum, or the Folklore Museum, to learn more about the history and the traditions of Crete.

Next, drive to Elafonisi, one of the most stunning and exotic beaches in Crete. Enjoy the crystal clear water, the soft white and pink sand, and the natural beauty of the lagoon and the island. You can also explore the nearby cedar forest, the sand dunes, and the rock formations, or visit the Agia Irini Monastery and the Chrysoskalitissa Monastery, to see some of the religious and historical sites of the area.

Day 2: Rethymnon and Balos

Start your day in Rethymnon, one of the most elegant and lively cities in Crete. Explore the beautiful old town, admire the Venetian and Ottoman architecture, and visit the majestic Fortezza and the Rimondi Fountain. You can also visit the Archaeological Museum, the Historical and Folklore Museum, or the Centre of Contemporary Art, to learn more about the history and the culture of Crete.

Next, drive to Balos, another spectacular and scenic beach in Crete. Take a boat from Kissamos or drive to the parking lot and hike to the beach, and marvel at the turquoise water, the white sand, and the rocky islet of Gramvousa. You can also swim, snorkel, or sunbathe, or visit the Gramvousa Castle and the Balos Lagoon, to see some of the natural and cultural attractions of the area.

Day 3: Heraklion and Knossos

Start your day in Heraklion, one of the most modern and vibrant cities in Crete. Visit the impressive Venetian fortress and the port, and stroll along the pedestrian street of 25th August. You can also visit the Archaeological Museum, the Historical Museum, or the Natural History Museum, to learn more about the history and the nature of Crete.

Next, drive to Knossos, one of the most famous and

fascinating archaeological sites in Crete. Explore the ancient palace of the Minoans, the oldest civilization in Europe, and admire the colorful frescoes, the intricate architecture, and the mysterious legends. You can also visit the nearby Archaeological Site of Malia, another important Minoan palace, or the Archaeological Site of Phaistos, another impressive Minoan settlement.

Day 4: Agios Nikolaos and Spinalonga

Start your day in Agios Nikolaos, one of the most picturesque and cosmopolitan towns in Crete. Enjoy the views of the lake and the bay, and visit the Folklore Museum, the Archaeological Museum, or the Cretan House, to learn more about the art and the life of Crete.

Next, take a boat to Spinalonga, one of the most intriguing and haunting islands in Crete. Explore the Venetian fortress and the leper colony, and learn about the history and the stories of the island. You can also swim, snorkel, or relax on the nearby beaches of Plaka, Elounda, or Kolokitha.

Day 5: Samaria Gorge and Sfakia

Start your day early and drive to the Omalos Plateau, where the entrance to the Samaria Gorge is located. Hike through the longest and most spectacular gorge in Europe, and admire the stunning scenery, the diverse flora and fauna, and the Iron Gates. You can also visit the abandoned village of Samaria, and the Agia Roumeli beach, where you can rest and refresh.

Next, take a ferry to Sfakia, one of the most traditional and authentic regions in Crete. Enjoy the views of the rugged mountains and the blue sea, and visit the villages of Chora Sfakion, Loutro, or Anopolis, where you can taste the local cuisine, such as the sfakian pies, the lamb with stamnagathi, or the honey with yogurt.

Chapter 12 • Travelling with Children

Child-Friendly Attractions

Crete is a wonderful destination for families, as it offers a variety of attractions and activities that are suitable and enjoyable for children of all ages. Below are some of the best child-friendly attractions that you can visit in Crete:

Beaches in Crete

One of the main attractions of Crete is its stunning coastline, with over 1,000 km of beaches to choose from. The island has some of the most beautiful and cleanest beaches in Europe, with crystal clear water, soft sand, and natural scenery. The beaches in Crete are also very child-friendly, as they are usually shallow, calm, and safe, and have plenty of facilities, such as sunbeds, umbrellas, showers, toilets, lifeguards, and water sports. Some of the best beaches for families in Crete are:

Elafonisi Beach: This is one of the most famous and exotic beaches in Crete, located in the southwest of the island. It is known for its pink sand, which is caused by the thousands of broken shells it contains, and its shallow turquoise water, which forms a lagoon between the mainland and the small island of Elafonisi. The beach is ideal for children, as they can play, swim, and explore the island, which is a protected nature reserve. The beach also has a snack bar, a souvenir shop, and a parking lot.

Balos Beach and Lagoon: This is another spectacular and scenic beach in Crete, located in the northwest of the island. It is accessible by boat from Kissamos port or by car and a short hike from the parking lot. The beach consists of white sand and shallow blue water, which surrounds the rocky islet of Gramvousa. The beach is perfect for children, as they can swim, snorkel, or relax in the lagoon, or visit the Gramvousa Castle and the Balos Lagoon, which are some of the natural and cultural attractions of the area.

Agia Pelagia Beach: This is one of the most popular and lively beaches in Crete, located in the north of the island, near Heraklion. It is a long sandy beach, with clear and calm water, and a variety of tourist facilities, such as hotels, restaurants, bars, shops, and water sports. The beach is great for children, as they can enjoy the water activities, such as kayaking, paddle boarding, or jet skiing, or join the kids' club, which offers games, crafts, and entertainment.

Museums in Crete

Another attraction of Crete is its rich and diverse cultural heritage, with a history that spans over 4,000 years. The museums in Crete are also very child-friendly, as they are interactive, educational, and entertaining, and have special programs, exhibits, and activities for children. Some of the best museums for families in Crete are:

Heraklion Archaeological Museum: This is one of the most important and impressive archaeological museums in Greece, located in the capital city of Heraklion. It displays the artifacts and the treasures of the Minoan civilization, the oldest civilization in Europe, which flourished on Crete from 3000 to 1450 BC. The museum has 27 galleries, covering various aspects of the Minoan culture, such as religion, art, economy, society, and daily life. The museum is ideal for children, as they can learn about the history and the myths of Crete, admire the colorful frescoes, the intricate jewelry, and the mysterious symbols, and participate in the workshops, the games, and the tours that the museum offers.

Aquaworld Aquarium and Reptile Rescue

Centre: This is one of the most fun and unique museums in Crete, located in the town of Hersonissos. It is the first aquarium and reptile rescue centre in Crete, which hosts a variety of marine and terrestrial animals, such as fish, turtles, snakes, lizards, crocodiles, and more. The museum is perfect for children, as they can see, touch, and learn about the animals, and even hold some of them, such as snakes and lizards. The museum also has a souvenir shop, a snack bar, and a playground.

Lychnostatis Open Air Museum: This is one of the most charming and authentic museums in Crete, located in the town of Hersonissos. It is an open-air museum, which recreates the traditional life and culture of Crete, with a collection of buildings, tools, crafts, and products. The museum has various sections, such as a farmhouse, a windmill, a chapel, a wine press, a herb garden, and a folk art gallery. The museum is wonderful for children, as they can experience the rural and natural environment of Crete, and join the activities, such as pottery, weaving, or baking, that the museum organizes.

Water Parks in Crete

One more attraction of Crete is its fun and exciting water parks, which are ideal for families who love water and adventure. The island has several water parks that offer a variety of slides, pools, rides, and games, for all ages and preferences. The water parks in Crete are also very child-friendly, as they have special areas, facilities, and staff for children, and they follow high standards of safety and hygiene. Some of the best water parks for families in Crete are:

Watercity Waterpark: This is one of the largest and most modern water parks in Crete, located in the village of Anopolis, near Heraklion. It has over 30 slides, pools, and attractions, such as the Kamikaze, the Black Hole, the Lazy River, and the Wave Pool. It also has a children's area, with a pirate ship, a castle, and a playground. The water park also has a restaurant, a snack bar, a souvenir shop, and a mini market.

Acqua Plus Water Park: This is another excellent and quality water park in Crete, located in the village of Hersonissos, near Heraklion. It has over 20 slides, pools, and attractions, such as the Spacebowl, the Hydrotube, the Crazy River, and the Tsunami. It also has a children's area, with a water playground, a mini slide, and a splash pool. The water park also has a restaurant, a snack bar, a souvenir shop, and a massage area.

Limnoupolis Water Park: This is another fun and entertaining water park in Crete, located in the village of

Varipetro, near Chania. It has over 10 slides, pools, and attractions, such as the Triple Twist, the Giant Slide, the Lazy River, and the Jacuzzi. It also has a children's area, with a water castle, a mini slide, and a splash pool. The water park also has a restaurant, a snack bar, a souvenir shop, and a mini golf.

Child-Friendly Accommodation

Below are some of the best child-friendly accommodation options that you can choose from in Crete:

Hotels and Resorts in Crete

Some of the best hotels and resorts for families in Crete are:

Grecotel Creta Palace: This is a 5-star beachfront hotel in the city of Rethymnon, with a stunning view of the sea and the mountains. It has spacious and elegant family rooms and bungalows, with balconies, terraces, or gardens. It also has a kids club, a playground, a kids pool, and a water park, with slides and fountains. It also offers various activities, such as sports, games, crafts, and shows, for children of all ages.

Kiani Beach Resort: This is a 4-star all-inclusive resort in the village of Kalyves, overlooking a sandy beach. It has cozy and modern family rooms and suites, with kitchenettes, balconies, or terraces. It also has a kids club, a playground, a kids pool, and a water park, with slides and a pirate ship. It also offers various activities, such as sports, games, crafts, and shows, for children of all ages.

Out of the Blue Resort and Spa: This is a 4-star resort in the village of Malia, surrounded by gardens and pools. It has luxurious and stylish family rooms and suites, with kitchenettes, balconies, or terraces. It also has a kids club, a playground, a kids pool, and a water park, with slides and a lazy river. It also offers various activities, such as sports, games, crafts, and shows, for children of all ages.

Villas and Apartments in Crete

Some of the best villas and apartments for families in Crete are:

Villa Kynthia: This is a charming and traditional villa in the village of Panormos, near the beach. It has four spacious and cozy bedrooms, a living room, a dining room, a kitchen, and a bathroom. It also has a garden, a terrace, and a pool, with sunbeds, umbrellas, and a barbecue. It also offers various amenities, such as air conditioning, Wi-Fi, TV, DVD, and books.

Casa Delfino Hotel and Spa: This is an elegant and historic hotel in the old town of Chania, near the harbor. It has six luxurious and spacious apartments, with one or two bedrooms, a living room, a kitchenette, and a bathroom. It also has a rooftop terrace, a spa, and a restaurant, with a view of the sea and the city. It also offers various amenities, such as air conditioning, Wi-Fi, TV, DVD, and books.

Agios Nikolaos General Hospital: This is a modern and comfortable apartment in the city of Agios Nikolaos, near the lake and the bay. It has two bright and cozy bedrooms, a living room, a kitchen, and a bathroom. It also has a balcony, a garden, and a parking lot, with a view of the sea and the mountains. It also offers various amenities, such as air conditioning, Wi-Fi, TV, DVD, and books.

Chapter 13 • Travelling on a Budget

Budget-Friendly Accommodation

Below are some of the best budget-friendly accommodation options that you can choose from in Crete:

Hostels in Crete

Some of the best hostels for travelers in Crete are:

Cocoon City Hostel: This is a modern and stylish hostel in the city of Heraklion, near the port and the center. It has spacious and clean dorms and private rooms, with air conditioning, lockers, and free Wi-Fi. It also has a lounge, a kitchen, a terrace, and a bar, where you can relax and socialize. It also offers various services, such as laundry, luggage storage, and bike rental. The price for a bed in a dorm starts from 15 euros per night.

Rethymno Youth Hostel: This is a cozy and traditional hostel in the old town of Rethymnon, near the beach and the fortress. It has simple and comfortable dorms and private rooms, with fans, lockers, and free Wi-Fi. It also has a garden, a patio, and a kitchen, where you can chill and mingle. It also offers various services, such as laundry, luggage storage, and tour booking. The price for a bed in a dorm starts from 12 euros per night.

Chania Hostel: This is a charming and historic hostel in the old town of Chania, near the harbor and the market. It has colorful and cozy dorms and private rooms, with air conditioning, lockers, and free Wi-Fi. It also has a lounge, a kitchen, a rooftop, and a bar, where you can enjoy and socialize. It also offers various services, such as laundry, luggage storage, and bike rental. The price for a bed in a dorm starts from 14 euros per night.

Campsites in Crete

Some of the best campsites for travelers in Crete are:

Camping Mithimna: This is a lovely and friendly campsite in the village of Platanias, near the beach and the river. It has spacious and shaded pitches and cabins, with electricity, water, and free Wi-Fi. It also has a restaurant, a bar, a mini market, and a playground, where you can eat, drink, and play. It also offers various services, such as laundry, luggage storage, and tour booking. The price for a pitch starts from 6 euros per night, and the price for a cabin starts from 25 euros per night.

Camping Paleochora: This is a beautiful and relaxing campsite in the town of Paleochora, near the beach and the center. It has large and green pitches and cabins, with electricity, water, and free Wi-Fi. It also has a snack bar, a mini market, and a library, where you can snack, shop, and read. It also offers various services, such as laundry, luggage storage, and bike rental. The price for a pitch starts from 5 euros per night, and the price for a cabin starts from 20 euros per night.

Camping No Problem: This is a fun and lively campsite in the village of Sisi, near the beach and the port. It has sunny and sandy pitches and cabins, with electricity, water, and free Wi-Fi. It also has a restaurant, a bar, and a pool, where you can dine, drink, and swim. It also offers various services, such as laundry, luggage storage, and car rental. The price for a pitch starts from 7 euros per night, and the price for a cabin starts from 30 euros per night.

Cheap Eats and Local Food

Below are some of the best cheap eats and local food that

you can enjoy in Crete:

Bougatsa

Bougatsa is a popular and tasty pastry that is eaten for breakfast or as a snack. It consists of thin layers of phyllo dough, filled with sweet cream or savory cheese, and sprinkled with sugar or cinnamon. Bougatsa is usually sold in bakeries or street stalls, and it is best eaten warm and fresh. You can find bougatsa all over Crete, but the most famous and original one is from Chania, where it is made with a special type of cheese called mizithra.

Dakos

Dakos is a simple and satisfying dish that is eaten as a starter or a light meal. It consists of a round barley rusk, topped with chopped tomatoes, crumbled feta cheese, oregano, and olive oil. Dakos is also known as koukouvagia or owl, because of its shape and color. Dakos is a typical dish of Crete, and it is a great way to use the dry and hard rusks, which are a staple of the Cretan diet. You can find dakos in most taverns and restaurants, or you can make it yourself with fresh and quality ingredients.

Kalitsounia

Kalitsounia are small and savory pies that are eaten as a

snack or a side dish. They are made with thin dough, filled with cheese, spinach, herbs, or honey, and baked or fried. Kalitsounia are a traditional and festive dish of Crete, and they are often served during Easter or other celebrations. You can find kalitsounia in bakeries or taverns, or you can buy them from street vendors, who sell them hot and crispy. You can also try different types of kalitsounia, such as sweet ones with cinnamon and sugar, or spicy ones with peppers and onions.

Souvlaki

Souvlaki is a famous and delicious dish that is eaten as a main course or a fast food. It consists of small pieces of meat, usually pork, chicken, or lamb, grilled on a skewer or a spit, and served with bread, salad, fries, and tzatziki sauce. Souvlaki is a common dish in Greece, but it is also very popular in Crete, where it is known as ovelias or lamb. You can find souvlaki in most taverns and restaurants, or you can buy it from street stalls or kiosks, where it is cheap and fresh. You can also order souvlaki wrapped in a pita bread, which is called gyros.

Raki

Raki is a strong and aromatic spirit that is drunk as an aperitif or a digestif. It is made from the distillation of grape pomace, which is the residue of the wine production. Raki is a traditional and symbolic drink of Crete, and it is often offered as a sign of friendship and hospitality. You can find raki in most taverns and bars, or you can buy it from local producers, who make it with their own grapes and herbs. You can also try different flavors of raki, such as honey, cinnamon, or anise.

Free and Affordable Attractions

Below are some of the best free and affordable attractions that you can visit in Crete:

Beaches in Crete

Some of the best beaches for travelers in Crete are:

Elafonisi Beach: This is one of the most famous and exotic beaches in Crete, located in the southwest of the island. It is known for its pink sand, which is caused by the thousands of broken shells it contains, and its shallow turquoise water, which forms a lagoon between the mainland and the small island of Elafonisi. The beach is ideal for travelers, as they can enjoy the natural beauty and the tranquility of the area. The beach also has a snack bar, a souvenir shop, and a parking lot.

Balos Beach and Lagoon: This is another spectacular and scenic beach in Crete, located in the northwest of the island. It is accessible by boat from Kissamos port or by car and a short hike from the parking lot. The beach consists of white sand and shallow blue water, which surrounds the rocky islet of Gramvousa. The beach is perfect for travelers, as they can marvel at the views and the wildlife of the area, such as dolphins, turtles, and birds. The beach also has a snack bar, a souvenir shop, and a parking lot.

Agia Pelagia Beach: This is one of the most popular and lively beaches in Crete, located in the north of the island, near Heraklion. It is a long sandy beach, with clear and calm water, and a variety of tourist facilities, such as hotels, restaurants, bars, shops, and water sports. The beach is great for travelers, as they can enjoy the water activities, such as kayaking, paddle boarding, or jet skiing, or join the events, such as parties, concerts, or festivals, that the beach hosts.

Museums in Crete

Some of the best museums for travelers in Crete are:

Heraklion Archaeological Museum: This is one of the most important and impressive archaeological museums in Greece, located in the capital city of Heraklion. It displays the artifacts and the treasures of the Minoan civilization, the oldest civilization in Europe, which flourished on Crete from 3000 to 1450 BC. The museum has 27 galleries, covering various aspects of the Minoan culture, such as religion, art, economy, society, and daily life. The museum is ideal for travelers, as they can learn about the history and the myths of Crete, admire the colorful frescoes, the intricate jewelry, and the mysterious symbols, and participate in the workshops, the games, and the tours that the museum offers. The admission fee is 10 euros, but it is free for students and children under 18.

Aquaworld Aquarium and Reptile Rescue Centre: This is one of the most fun and unique museums in Crete, located in the town of Hersonissos. It is the first aquarium and reptile rescue centre in Crete, which hosts a variety of marine and terrestrial animals, such as fish, turtles, snakes, lizards, crocodiles, and more. The museum is perfect for travelers, as they can see, touch, and learn about the animals, and even hold some of them, such as snakes and lizards. The museum also has a souvenir shop, a snack bar, and a playground. The admission fee is 9 euros, but it is free for children under 5.

Lychnostatis Open Air Museum: This is one of the most charming and authentic museums in Crete, located in the town of Hersonissos. It is an open-air museum, which recreates the traditional life and culture of Crete, with a collection of buildings, tools, crafts, and products. The museum has various sections, such as a farmhouse, a windmill, a chapel, a wine press, a herb garden, and a folk art gallery. The museum is wonderful for travelers, as they can experience the rural and natural environment of Crete, and join the activities, such as pottery, weaving, or baking, that the museum organizes. The admission fee is 5 euros, but it is free for children under 12.

Hikes and Walks in Crete

Some of the best hikes and walks for travelers in Crete are:

Samaria Gorge: This is one of the most famous and spectacular hikes in Crete, located in the southwest of the island. It is the longest and most beautiful gorge in Europe, with a length of 16 km, and a depth of up to 500 m. The hike starts from the Omalos Plateau, and ends at the Agia Roumeli beach, passing through stunning scenery, diverse flora and fauna, and the Iron Gates. The hike is ideal for travelers, as they can enjoy the challenge and the reward of the hike, and admire the views and the wildlife of the area, such as kri-kri, eagles, and flowers. The hike is open from May to October, and the entrance fee is 5 euros, but it is free for children under 15.

Rethymnon Old Town: This is one of the most elegant and lively walks in Crete, located in the old town of Rethymnon, near the beach and the fortress. It is a walk through the history and the culture of Crete, with a mix of Venetian and Ottoman architecture, and a variety of sights and attractions. The walk starts from the majestic Fortezza, and ends at the Rimondi Fountain, passing through beautiful streets, squares, churches, mosques, and museums. The walk is perfect for travelers, as they can explore the charm and the atmosphere of the old town, and visit the sights and the attractions of the area, such as the Archaeological Museum, the Historical and Folklore Museum, or the Centre of Contemporary Art. The walk is open all year round, and most of the sights and attractions are free or have low admission fees.

Seitan Limania Beach: This is one of the most fun and adventurous walks in Crete, located in the northeast of the island, near Chania. It is a walk to a hidden and stunning beach, with turquoise water, white sand, and rocky cliffs. The walk starts from the parking lot, and ends at the beach, passing through a narrow and steep path, with some rocks and steps. The walk is wonderful for travelers, as they can enjoy the thrill and the surprise of the walk, and marvel at the views and the beauty of the beach. The walk is open all year round, but it is best to avoid it in rainy or windy days, as it can be slippery and dangerous. The walk is free to enter, and the beach has no facilities, so it is advisable to bring water, food, and sunscreen.

Transportation Tips for Saving Money

Below are some of the best transportation tips for saving money in Crete:

Rent a Car in Crete

One of the best ways to get around Crete is to rent a car, as it gives you the freedom and flexibility to visit any place and any time you want. However, renting a car in Crete can also be costly, depending on the type, the season, and the duration of your rental. Therefore, below are some tips to save money on car rental in Crete:

Book in advance: Booking your car rental online and in advance can help you find the best deals and discounts, as well as secure the availability and the quality of your car. You can use comparison websites to find the cheapest and most reliable car rental companies in Crete.

Choose a small and economical car: Choosing a small and economical car can help you save money on fuel, tolls, and parking fees, as well as avoid any extra charges for large or luxury cars. You can also opt for a manual transmission, which is usually cheaper and more common than an automatic one in Crete.

Avoid the airport and the port: Picking up and dropping off your car at the airport or the port can incur additional fees and taxes, as well as higher prices and lower availability. Therefore, it is better to choose a car rental location in the city or the town, where you can find cheaper and more convenient options. You can also use public transport or a taxi to get to and from the airport or the port, which is usually cheaper and faster than renting a car there.

Check the insurance and the extras: Before you rent a car in Crete, make sure you check the insurance and the extras that are included or excluded in your rental agreement. You may want to avoid any unnecessary or excessive insurance or extras, such as GPS, child seats, or additional drivers, which can increase your rental cost. You may also want to check your own travel insurance or credit card coverage, which may already cover some or all of the car rental insurance in Crete.

Use Public Transport in Crete

Another way to get around Crete is to use public transport, which is fairly decent and cheap, especially in the north part of the island. However, public transport in Crete can also be limited and infrequent, especially in the south and the east of the island, where buses only run twice a day or less. Therefore, below are some tips to make the most of public transport in Crete:

Plan ahead: Planning your itinerary and your schedule in advance can help you find the best routes and timetables for public transport in Crete, as well as avoid any delays or missed connections. You can use online tools to find the bus schedules and fares in Crete, or ask the local tourist offices or your accommodation for more information and advice.

Buy tickets in advance: Buying your bus tickets in advance can help you secure your seat and your price, as well as avoid any queues or hassles at the bus stations. You can buy your bus tickets online, at the bus stations, or at some kiosks or travel agencies in Crete. You can also buy a return ticket, which is usually cheaper and more convenient than buying two single tickets.

Travel off-peak: Traveling off-peak can help you save money and time on public transport in Crete, as well as enjoy a more comfortable and less crowded ride. You can avoid traveling during the peak hours, which are usually from 7 am to 9 am and from 5 pm to 7 pm, or during the peak seasons, which are usually from June to September and from December to January. You can also take advantage of the off-peak discounts and deals, which are usually offered by some bus companies in Crete.

Take a Ferry in Crete

One more way to get around Crete is to take a ferry, which is a fun and scenic way to travel between the mainland and the islands, or between the different ports and towns in Crete. However, taking a ferry in Crete can also be pricey and slow, depending on the type, the season, and the duration of your trip. Therefore, below are some tips to save money on ferry travel in Crete:

Book in advance: Booking your ferry ticket online and in advance can help you find the best deals and discounts, as well as secure the availability and the quality of your seat. You can use comparison websites to find the cheapest and most reliable ferry companies and routes in Crete.

Choose a standard and slow ferry: Choosing a standard and slow ferry can help you save money on your ticket price, as well as enjoy the views and the atmosphere of the sea. You can avoid the fast and luxurious ferries, which are usually more expensive and less frequent than the regular ones. You can also opt for a deck seat, which is usually cheaper and more spacious than a cabin seat.

Travel off-peak: Traveling off-peak can help you save money and time on ferry travel in Crete, as well as enjoy a more comfortable and less crowded ride. You can avoid traveling during the peak hours, which are usually from 9 am to 11 am and from 4 pm to 6 pm, or during the peak seasons, which are usually from June to September and from December to January. You can also take advantage of the off-peak discounts and deals, which are usually offered by some ferry companies in Crete.

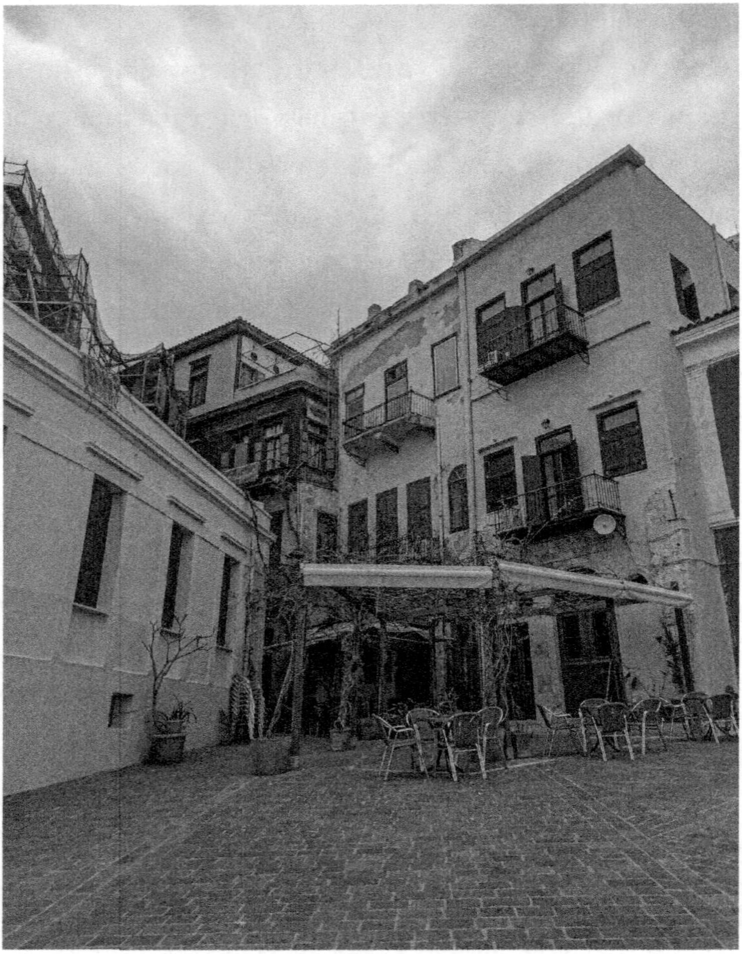

Chapter 14 • Day Trips and Excursions

Santorini

Santorini is one of the most iconic and famous Greek islands, with its stunning caldera, white villages, blue domes, and breathtaking sunsets. It is also one of the most popular and convenient day trip destinations from Crete, as it is only a short ferry ride away from the largest and most diverse island in Greece. However, visiting Santorini in one day can also be challenging and expensive, as it is a large and crowded island, with many attractions and activities to explore and enjoy. Therefore, below are some tips and suggestions to help you plan your Santorini day trip from Crete, and make the most of your time and money on this unique and beautiful island.

How to Get to Santorini from Crete

The easiest and fastest way to get to Santorini from Crete is by ferry, which takes about 2.5 hours, depending on the type and the route of the ferry. There are several ferry companies that operate daily or weekly services between Crete and Santorini. You can book your ferry tickets online, at the port, or at some travel agencies in Crete, and you can choose between economy or business class seats, or cabins. The price for a one-way ferry ticket starts from 40 euros, but it can vary depending on the season, the availability, and the demand.

The main departure port in Crete is Heraklion, which is the capital and the largest city of the island, located in the north-central part of Crete. You can get to Heraklion by car, bus, taxi, or plane, from any part of Crete, and you can find plenty of facilities, services, and attractions in the city, such as hotels, restaurants, shops, museums, and monuments. The main arrival port in Santorini is Athinios, which is the main commercial and passenger port of the island, located in the south-west part of Santorini. You can get to Athinios by bus, taxi, or car, from any part of Santorini, and you can find some facilities, services, and attractions near the port, such as hotels, restaurants, shops, and viewpoints.

What to See and Do in Santorini in One Day

Santorini is a large and diverse island, with many attractions and activities to suit every taste and interest. However, if you only have one day to explore Santorini, you can still enjoy some of the highlights and get a glimpse of the beauty and culture of the island. Below is a suggested itinerary for one day in Santorini, based on the most popular and convenient destinations and experiences:

Start your day in Fira, which is the capital and the largest town of Santorini, located in the center of the island, on the edge of the caldera. Wander around the picturesque and lively streets, admire the whitewashed houses and the blue domes, and visit some of the sights and attractions of the town, such as the Archaeological Museum, the Folklore Museum, or the Cable Car. You can also enjoy the stunning views of the caldera, the volcano, and the sea, from the many terraces, cafes, and bars that line the cliff.

Next, take a bus, a taxi, or a car to Oia, which is the most famous and scenic village of Santorini, located in the north-west of the island, on the tip of the caldera. Explore the charming and romantic streets, admire the elegant houses and the colorful doors, and visit some of the sights and attractions of the village, such as the Maritime Museum, the Castle of Agios Nikolaos, or the Church of Panagia Platsani. You can also enjoy the breathtaking views of the caldera, the volcano, and the sea, from the many terraces, cafes, and bars that line the cliff.

Then, take a bus, a taxi, or a car to Perissa, which is one of the most beautiful and popular beaches of Santorini, located in the south-east of the island, on the opposite side of the caldera. Enjoy the black volcanic sand, the clear blue water, and the natural scenery of the beach, and relax, swim, or sunbathe on the sunbeds and umbrellas that are available for rent. You can also enjoy the water sports, such as windsurfing, jet skiing, or snorkeling, that are offered on the beach, or visit some of the sights and attractions near the beach, such as the Ancient Thera, the Mesa Vouno, or the Church of Timios Stavros.

Finally, take a bus, a taxi, or a car back to Oia, and watch the sunset, which is one of the most famous and spectacular attractions of Santorini, and one of the most memorable experiences of your trip. Find a spot on the caldera, the castle, or the church, and marvel at the changing colors of the sky, the sea, and the houses, as the sun dips into the horizon. You can also enjoy the sunset from a boat, a restaurant, or a bar, and experience the romantic and magical atmosphere of the island.

Kythira

Kythira is a small and serene island, located between the Peloponnese and Crete, at the crossroads of the Aegean, the Ionian, and the Cretan seas. It is an ideal island for travelers who seek a tranquil and authentic escape from the crowds and the noise of the more popular Greek islands. It has a diverse and beautiful landscape, with rocky cliffs, sandy beaches, lush forests, and cascading waterfalls. It also has a rich and varied cultural heritage, with influences from the Venetians, the Ottomans, the British, and the mainland Greeks. It is also the mythical birthplace of Aphrodite, the goddess of love and beauty, according to some legends. Kythira is a great day trip destination from Crete, as it is only a short ferry ride away from the largest and most diverse island in Greece. However, visiting Kythira in one day can also be challenging and rewarding, as it is a large and secluded island, with many attractions and activities to explore and enjoy. Therefore, below are some tips and suggestions to help you plan your Kythira day trip from Crete, and make the most of your time and money on this hidden gem of an island.

How to Get to Kythira from Crete

The easiest and fastest way to get to Kythira from Crete is by ferry, which takes about 2 hours, depending on the type and the route of the ferry. There are several ferry companies that operate daily or weekly services between Crete and Kythira. You can book your ferry tickets online, at the port, or at some travel agencies in Crete, and you can choose between economy or business class seats, or cabins. The price for a one-way ferry ticket starts from 40 euros, but it can vary depending on the season, the availability, and the demand.

The main departure port in Crete is Heraklion, which is the capital and the largest city of the island, located in the north-central part of Crete. You can get to Heraklion by car, bus, taxi, or plane, from any part of Crete, and you can find plenty of facilities, services, and attractions in the city, such as hotels, restaurants, shops, museums, and monuments. The main arrival port in Kythira is Diakofti, which is the main commercial and passenger port of the island, located in the south-east of the island. You can get to Diakofti by bus, taxi, or car, from any part of Kythira, and you can find some facilities, services, and attractions near the port, such as hotels, restaurants, shops, and viewpoints.

What to See and Do in Kythira in One Day

Kythira is a large and diverse island, with many attractions and activities to suit every taste and interest. However, if you only have one day to explore Kythira, you can still enjoy some of the highlights and get a glimpse of the beauty and culture of the island. Below is a suggested itinerary for one day in Kythira, based on the most popular and convenient destinations and experiences:

Start your day in Chora, which is the capital and the largest town of Kythira, located in the south of the island, on the edge of a cliff. Wander around the picturesque and quiet streets, admire the whitewashed houses and the colorful doors, and visit some of the sights and attractions of the town, such as the Venetian Castle, the Archaeological Museum, or the Church of Panagia Myrtidiotissa. You can also enjoy the stunning views of the sea and the island, from the many terraces, cafes, and bars that line the cliff.

Next, take a bus, a taxi, or a car to Kapsali, which is a small and scenic seaside village, located in the south of the island, below Chora. Enjoy the sandy beach, the clear water, and the natural scenery of the village, and relax, swim, or sunbathe on the sunbeds and umbrellas that are available for rent. You can also enjoy the water sports, such as kayaking, paddle boarding, or snorkeling, that are offered on the beach, or visit some of the sights and attractions near the village, such as the Lighthouse, the Monastery of Agios Ioannis, or the Islet of Chytra.

Then, take a bus, a taxi, or a car to Mylopotamos, which is a charming and green village, located in the west of the island, on the slopes of a mountain. Explore the traditional and authentic streets, admire the stone houses and the flower gardens, and visit some of the sights and attractions of the village, such as the Watermill Museum, the Venetian Bridge, or the Church of Agia Sofia. You can also enjoy the natural beauty and the tranquility of the area, and visit some of the nearby waterfalls, such as Neraida, Fonissa, or Kalami.

Finally, take a bus, a taxi, or a car back to Diakofti, and watch the sunset, which is one of the most beautiful and romantic attractions of Kythira, and one of the most memorable experiences of your trip. Find a spot on the beach, the port, or the hill, and marvel at the changing colors of the sky, the sea, and the island, as the sun dips into the horizon. You can also enjoy the sunset from a boat, a restaurant, or a bar, and experience the peaceful and magical atmosphere of the island.

Elounda

Elounda is a charming fishing village on the eastern coast of Crete, Greece. It is a perfect destination for a relaxing day trip, away from the crowds and noise of the bigger resorts. Elounda offers a variety of attractions and activities for visitors of all ages and interests. Below are some of the highlights of Elounda as a day trip destination:

Enjoy the scenic views of the Mirabello Bay and the island of Spinalonga, a former leper colony and Venetian fortress. You can take a boat trip to Spinalonga and explore its history and culture, or admire it from the shore.

Visit the Sunken City of Olous, an ancient Greek city that was submerged by the sea. You can see some of the ruins underwater, or walk along the coastal path that leads to the site.

Relax on the sandy beaches of Elounda, such as the main beach near the harbour, or the quieter ones on the Kolokytha Peninsula. You can swim, sunbathe, or try some water sports, such as snorkeling, kayaking, or windsurfing.

Taste the delicious local cuisine at one of the

many tavernas and restaurants in Elounda. You can sample fresh seafood, traditional dishes, such as moussaka and souvlaki, or international options, such as pizza and burgers. Don't forget to try the local wine and raki, a strong spirit made from grapes.

Explore the charming streets and shops of Elounda, where you can find souvenirs, handicrafts, jewelry, and more. You can also visit the church of Agios Nikolaos, which has a beautiful mosaic floor, or the windmills that dot the landscape.

Take a ride on the little blue train, a fun and convenient way to see the countryside and villages around Elounda. You can choose from different routes and durations, and enjoy the panoramic views and commentary along the way.

Elounda is a hidden gem on the island of Crete, where you can experience the authentic Greek lifestyle and culture. It is a place where you can relax, have fun, and learn something new. Whether you are looking for history, nature, or adventure, Elounda has something for everyone. Book your day trip to Elounda and discover its beauty and charm.

Chapter 15 • Sustainability and Responsible Travel

Crete, the largest and most populous of the Greek islands, is a popular destination for travellers who seek sun, sea, and culture. However, Crete is also a place of rich biodiversity, ancient history, and diverse traditions, which deserve to be preserved and respected. That is why sustainable tourism, also known as ecotourism, is becoming more and more important for the island and its visitors.

Sustainable tourism is defined as responsible travel to natural areas that conserves the environment, sustains the well-being of the local people, and involves interpretation and education. This means that tourists who choose to travel sustainably aim to have a low impact on the environment, support the local communities, and learn about the nature and culture of the places they visit.

Eco-friendly Accommodations in Crete

One of the first steps to travel sustainably is to choose an accommodation that operates on an ecologically-friendly basis. In Crete, there are several options for eco-conscious travellers who want to stay in harmony with nature and support the local economy.

Some hotels in Crete have been awarded the Green Key, which is an eco-label for tourism and leisure establishments that are recognized for their sustainable operations. These hotels follow strict criteria regarding environmental management, water and energy consumption, waste management, green purchasing, and staff and guest involvement. Some examples of Green Key hotels in Crete are the Creta Maris Beach Resort, the Grecotel Creta Palace, and the Cretan Malia Park.

Another option for eco-friendly accommodation is to stay in a traditional stone-built house or villa, which have been restored and renovated using local materials and techniques. These houses offer a unique and authentic experience of the Cretan rural life, while also contributing to the preservation of the architectural heritage and the income of the local families. Some of these houses are also equipped with solar panels, organic gardens, and recycling facilities, to further reduce their environmental impact. Pure Crete is a company that specializes in renting such houses and villas, and has also been awarded the 4 Star Status for

Sustainable Tourism by AITO.

Eco-friendly Activities in Crete

Crete is a paradise for nature lovers, as it boasts a variety of landscapes, from the majestic mountains and gorges to the pristine beaches and islands. There are many ways to explore and enjoy the natural beauty of Crete, while also respecting and protecting it.

One of the most popular and rewarding activities is hiking, which allows you to discover the hidden gems of the island, such as the famous Samaria Gorge, the longest and deepest gorge in Europe, the Balos Lagoon, a stunning beach with turquoise waters, and the Lassithi Plateau, a fertile valley surrounded by mountains. Hiking is also a great way to learn about the flora and fauna of Crete, which include endemic and endangered species, such as the Cretan wild goat, the Cretan spiny mouse, and the Cretan dittany. There are many hiking trails and routes for all levels of difficulty and interest, and some of them are part of the European Natura 2000 network, which aims to protect the biodiversity and habitats of the continent.

Another eco-friendly activity that you can enjoy in Crete is cycling, which is not only a fun and healthy way to get around, but also a low-carbon and low-cost alternative to driving. Cycling can help you explore the countryside, the villages, and the coast of Crete, while also reducing your environmental footprint and supporting the local businesses. There are many bike rental shops and tour operators that offer bikes, equipment, and guided tours for cyclists of all ages and abilities. Some of the best places to cycle in Crete are the Apokoronas region, the Rethymno prefecture, and the Heraklion area.

If you are looking for a more adventurous and thrilling activity, you can try rafting, kayaking, or canyoning, which are some of the best ways to experience the rivers, lakes, and waterfalls of Crete. These activities are suitable for all seasons, as the water temperature and level vary throughout the year, creating different challenges and sceneries. You can also combine these activities with other outdoor sports, such as climbing, rappelling, or zip-lining, for a more exhilarating experience. Some of the best places to enjoy these activities are the Kourtaliotis River, the Preveli Lake, and the Ha Gorge.

Local Conservation Efforts in Crete

Sustainable tourism is not only about the choices and actions of the travellers, but also about the initiatives and efforts of the local people and organizations, who are the guardians and stewards of their land and culture. In Crete, there are many examples of local conservation efforts that aim to protect and promote the natural and cultural heritage of the island.

One of these efforts is the Cretan Olive Oil Network, which is a network of olive oil producers, cooperatives, and associations that work together to produce and market high-quality extra virgin olive oil, while also preserving the traditional and organic farming methods, the biodiversity of the olive groves, and the cultural identity of the olive oil sector. The network also organizes agrotourism and food tourism activities, such as olive oil tastings, workshops, and festivals, to educate and engage the visitors and the locals about the importance and benefits of olive oil.

Another local conservation effort is the Archelon, which is the Sea Turtle Protection Society of Greece, and has been active in Crete since 1983. The main goal of the society is to monitor and protect the nesting beaches of the loggerhead sea turtle, which is an endangered species that nests on the sandy shores of Crete, especially on the north coast. The society also runs rescue and rehabilitation centers for injured or sick turtles, and conducts awareness and education campaigns for the public and the authorities. The society also welcomes volunteers and supporters who want to help with the conservation work and learn more about the sea turtles.

Conclusion

Crete is a destination that offers something for everyone. Whether you are looking for ancient history, stunning nature, vibrant culture, or delicious cuisine, you will find it on this island. Crete is the largest and most diverse of the Greek islands, with a rich heritage that spans from the Minoan civilization to the modern day. You can explore the impressive palaces of Knossos and Phaestos, the charming Venetian harbours of Hania and Rethymno, the majestic mountains and gorges of the interior, and the idyllic beaches and islands of the coast.

You can also immerse yourself in the local traditions, music, art, and festivals that reflect the Cretan spirit of hospitality and resilience. And you can taste the flavours of the Mediterranean diet, with fresh seafood, olive oil, cheese, wine, and herbs that make every meal a delight.

Crete is a place that will inspire you, challenge you, and reward you. It is a place that you will want to return to again and again, discovering new aspects and experiences each time. Crete is not just an island, it is a world of its own.

Printed in Great Britain
by Amazon